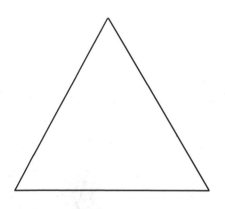

DARK SIDE OF THE
MOON REVEALED

BRIAN SOUTHALL

First Published 2013 by Clarksdale Books

Text © Brian Southall 2013
This work © Ovolo Books Ltd

Paperback ISBN: 978 1 9059 5998 3

Printed in the UK

For more information visit: www.clarksdalebooks.co.uk
Clarksdale is an imprint of Ovolo Books Ltd

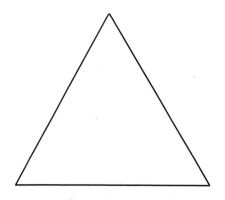

DARK SIDE OF THE
MOON REVEALED

BRIAN SOUTHALL

DSOM Who's Who?

Chris Adamso

The long time road manager and production manager for Pink Floyd who appeared on *Dark Side of the Moon* and has been credited with coming up with the song title Any Colour You Like . Pink Anderson - American bluesman born in South Carolina in 1900 (died in 1974), recorded for the Riverside and Prestige labels and gave half his name to Pink Floyd.

Michelangelo Antonioni

Italian film director who made successful hip movie *Blow Up* (starring David Hemmings) in 1966 and then the commercial flop *Zabriskie Point* in 1970 which featured three Pink Floyd songs on the soundtrack.

Mike Appleton

BBC director/producer of the influential TV music programmes *The Old Grey Whistle Test* and *In Concert*.

Syd Barrett

Born Roger Keith Barrett in Cambridge in January 1946, he was a founding member of Pink Floyd in 1966 and wrote their early hits, but drug problems forced him to leave the band in 1968. He died in Cambridge in 2006.

Joe Boyd

American producer who was production manager of the Newport Jazz Festival in 1965, ran Elektra Records' London office and launched the UFO underground club before producing Pink Floyd's first recordings.

Billy Corgan
Founder and lead singer of American band The Smashing Pumpkins who inducted Pink Floyd into the US Rock 'n' Roll Hall of Fame in 1996 and performed with them at the ceremony.

Floyd Council
Born in North Carolina in 1911 (and died in 1976), he was known as Dipper Boy and recorded for ARC. He inspired Syd Barrett to take half of his name to go with Pink.

Al Coury
Capitol Records promotion executive who pushed for a single to support *Dark Side of the Moon* in America.

Clive Davis
New York-born lawyer who became head of CBS's Columbia Records, and who signed Blood Sweat & Tears, Janis Joplin and Santana ahead of securing Pink Floyd. He was dismissed from the label in 1973 accused of financial misdemeanours, but later founded the Arista record label.

Dan Davis
Capitol Records' head of creative services during the 1970s.

Chris Dennis
Cambridge musician and member of the Royal Air Force who was the frontman in the pre-Floyd band The Abdabs until 1964.

Lesley Duncan
A session singer and songwriter – she wrote Love Song for Elton John's *Tumbleweed Connection* album - who also made half a dozen solo albums and worked as a backing vocalist on DSOM.

Ian Emes
Award-winning filmmaker who created animation for Pink Floyd tracks on *Meddle* and *Dark Side of the Moon*.

Bob Ezrin
Canadian record producer for Pink Floyd and also Alice Cooper, Poco, Lou Reed, Peter Gabriel and Kiss.

John Fiddler
Member of the duo Medicine Head – with Peter Hope-Evans - who issued their own album called *Dark Side of the Moon* in 1972, a year before Pink Floyd's.

Bob Geldof
Singer with Irish punk band the Boomtown Rats from 1975 who starred as Pink in Pink Floyd's 1982 film version of *The Wall*. Organised Live Aid in 1985 and was involved in Floyd reforming for his Live8 concert in 2005.

David Gilmour
Born in Cambridge in March 1946, he studied at Cambridge Technical College with Syd Barrett before joining The Ramblers and Jokers Wild. He joined Floyd in January 1968, four months before Barrett's departure from the group.

Jeff Griffin
BBC Radio producer who oversaw the *In Concert* series and *Sounds of the Seventies* shows which featured Floyd tracks. He was the BBC's co-ordinator for Live Aid in 1985.

Loyd Grossman
American celebrity chef and broadcaster who worked as a music

reviewer for Rolling Stone magazine in the early 1970s.

James Guthrie

English engineer/producer who worked with Floyd from 1978 and remixed and re-mastered the 1993 and 2003 reissues of *Dark Side of the Moon*.

George Hardie

A distinguished artist who worked with the Hipgnosis team on the cover artwork for *Dark Side of the Moon*.

Roy Harper

British folk singer and songwriter, he was on the Harvest label for ten years from 1970. He formed a close relationship with Pink Floyd and appeared on both the group's albums and members' solo works.

Bob Harris

Co-founder of Time Out, and radio and TV music presenter who hosted *Sounds of the Seventies* and *The Old Grey Whistle Test* and went on to front shows on BBC Radios 1 and 2 and BBC 6Music.

Peter Jenner

Former London School of Economics lecturer who set up Blackhill Enterprises in order to manager Pink Floyd and also Roy Harper whose albums he produced. When Syd Barrett left Floyd, he continued to manage the former band member as a solo artist.

Malcolm Jones

EMI executive who was put in charge of launching the company's 'underground' label Harvest in 1969 which recruited Pink Floyd the following year.

Andrew King

Went to Westminster Public School with Peter Jenner and was his partner and chief financial backer in Blackhill Enterprises, which also involved Pink Floyd as partners, and which folded in the 1980s

Bob Klose

A former Cambridge schoolboy and guitarist with local band Blues Anonymous, he joined The Tea Set in 1964 and left a year later.

Paul McCartney

The man who was in The Beatles until 1970, visited Pink Floyd in sessions at Abbey Road studios and left some taped (but unused) answers to Roger Waters' *Dark Side of the Moon* question cards.

Gered Mankowitz

Son of leading writer Wolf Mankowtiz, he photographed The Rolling Stones on tour in the US in 1965 before working with a host of acts including Jimi Hendrix, Kate Bush, Leonard Cohen and Oasis.

Phil Manzanera

After a spell as a sound engineer, he joined Roxy Music as the band's guitarist in 1972, replacing one-time Floyd stand-in David O'List.

George Martin

The legendary producer of The Beatles opened his own AIR Studios in 1965 and employed producer Chris Thomas who, during 1973, worked with both Pink Floyd and Roxy Music.

Nick Mason

Founder member of Pink Floyd. Born in Birmingham in January 1944, he attended Regent Street Polytechnic in London to study architecture where he met Roger Waters and Rick Wright. They joined college band Sigma 6 which had been formed by two other students (and a sister) and soon after became known as The Abdabs (and occasionally The Screaming Abdabs) and later the Tea Set.

Bhaskar Menon

A leading record executive, he was head of Capitol Records in America from 1972 until 1977 when he was appointed as chairman of EMI Music Worldwide.

Bob Mercer

The Managing Director of EMI Records Group Repertoire Division from 1973, he worked closely with the company's roster of major British acts including Pink Floyd, Kate Bush, Queen, Sex Pistols, Paul McCartney and Rolling Stones. He died in 2010.

Clive Metcalfe

A student at the Regent Street Poly, he was an original member of Sigma 6 but left in 1964.

Nick Mobbs

The general manager of the Harvest label from 1972, he became head of EMI's A&R (Artists & Repertoire) department and memorably signed the Sex Pistols in 1976.

Bryan Morrison

A booking agent who also managed The Pretty Things, Fairport Convention and T Rex. He funded the first Pink Floyd recordings, booked their early club dates and also oversaw music publishing for them and other groups including Wham! He died in 2008 following a polo accident.

Pete Murray

A long-time BBC television and radio presenter who hosted both *Six-Five Special* and *Top of the Pops.*

Martin Nelson

Joined EMI in 1972 in special promotions and went on to work for CBS Records and Universal Music.

Keith Noble

An original member of the London-based group Sigma 6 who left to work with Clive Metcalfe

Sheila Noble

The sister of Keith, she appeared with Sigma 6 as a part-time vocalist.

Gerry O'Driscoll

A genial jack of all trades at Abbey Road where he helped out in the studios. He was recruited by Pink Floyd to contribute some memorable words to *Dark Side of the Moon.*

David O'List

Guitarist with The Nice on a 1967 tour with Jimi Hendrix, The Move and Pink Floyd. He stood in for Syd Barrett when he failed to appear and later joined Roxy Music.

Steve O'Rourke

He worked for Bryan Morrison as an agent before taking over as the manager of Pink Floyd in 1968. He remained in this role with the band, right up until his death in 2003.

Alan Parker

Film director who made *Midnight Express, Bugsy Malone* and *The*

Commitments, and who also turned *The Wall* into a cult movie in 1982.

Dick Parry
Renowned session musician who played saxophone on Pink Floyd's concert tours, as well as on their *Dark Side of the Moon* and *Wish You Were Here* albums.

Alan Parsons
Engineer and producer who worked with The Beatles at Abbey Road and was an engineer on their final live 'concert' on the roof of Apple's Savile Row offices in 1969. After engineering *Dark Side of the Moon* he produced Cockney Rebel and Pilot before forming the Alan Parsons Project.

Rupert Perry
A former A&R executive at Capitol Records in Los Angeles, he became president of EMI-America, head of EMI Records UK and also chairman of the British Phonographic Industry.

Roland Petit
Choreographer with the French ballet company Ballets de Marseilles, he invited Floyd to appear with his dancers in Marseille and Paris in 1971 and 1972.

Aubrey Powell
Designer from Cambridge who co-founded the Hipgnosis company, which created the artwork for Pink Floyd albums from 1968 until 1980.

Mark Rye
Former Harvest radio plugger who took over as label chief in 1974.

Polly Samson

The wife of David Gilmour – they married in 1994 – she co-wrote lyrics for Floyd's album of the same year, The Division Bell.

Gerald Scarfe

The cartoonist husband of actress Jane Asher, he produced animation for Floyd's *Wish You Were Here* tour and designed the album cover and the stage animations for *The Wall*.

Barbet Schroeder

Iranian-born film director who made the hippy culture movies More and *The Valley*, both of which both featured soundtrack music from Pink Floyd.

Terry Slater

Executive with both EMI Music Publishing and EMI Records, he went to school with Floyd's manager Steve O'Rourke.

Norman Smith

EMI staff engineer and producer who worked on The Beatles' first ever recording at Abbey Road in 1962. He produced the Floyd's single See Emily Play, as well as their albums, before going off to become the hit singer Hurricane Smith. He died in 2008.

Barry St John

Born in Scotland as Elizabeth Thompson, she signed recording deals with Decca, Columbia (one hit in 1965 with 'Come Away Melinda') and Major Minor before electing to work as a session singer with Roxy Music, Elton John and Pink Floyd.

Steve Stollman

Brother of American ESP Records chief Bernard, he helped put on the Spontaneous Underground shows at the Marquee Club.

Lisa Strike
Session singer on Floyd albums and tours who also backed Elton John, Leo Sayer, Bryan Ferry and Carly Simon.

Chris Thomas
Brought into 'supervise the mixing' on *Dark Side of the Moon* for a one-off payment, he had previously worked with The Beatles and produced albums for Procol Harum, Roxy Music, the Sex Pistols, Elton John and Paul McCartney.

Storm Thorgerson
A founding partner of the design company Hipgnosis, after it folded in 1983, he established his Storm Studio and designed further covers for Pink Floyd and also a solo album for David Gilmour.

Clare Torry
Session singer who performed vocals on the Floyd's 'Great Gig in the Sky', for which she was eventually awarded a composer's credit. She later sang the theme song for the TV series *Butterflies*, and worked with Culture Club and Meatloaf.

Ken Townsend
Long standing Abbey Road sound engineer – and eventually general manager – who worked on Beatles albums from *Rubber Soul* to *Sgt Pepper*, and who in 1966 invented ADT (automatic double tracking).

Doris Troy
US soul singer who hit the US top ten with 'Just One Look' and UK charts with 'Whatcha Gonna Do About It' before being signed to

The Beatles' Apple label in 1969, before contributing vocals to *Dark Side of the Moon*. She died in 2004.

Roger Waters

Guitar player turned bassist who was an original member of Pink Floyd – from the days of Sigma 6 – and who took over the creative reins from Syd Barrett in 1968. He eventually left the band in 1985, and mounted an acrimonious legal battle over the name Pink Floyd. Pete Watts – Road manger and sound engineer for Pink Floyd who died in 1976 and can be heard as one of the voices on *Dark Side of the Moon*.

L.G. (Leonard) Wood

Managing director of EMI Records who oversaw the signing of the company's impressive roster of British acts during the 1960s – including The Beatles and Pink Floyd.

Rick Wright

Keyboard player who joined Sigma 6 in 1963 as an occasional piano player and stayed with Pink Floyd from 1966 until his death in 2008, despite being relegated to the status of salaried member for almost the last thirty years of his life.

Walter Yetnikoff

Legendary volatile American record executive who inherited Pink Floyd when he took over as head of CBS Columbia label after the sacking of Clive Davis.

Don Zimmermann

Capitol's sales and promo Vice-President in 1973 who later became President of Capitol Records.

An Introduction

I first spoke to David Gilmour about *Dark Side of the Moon* in late 1981 – nearly a decade after the album was released to a hard core of fans eagerly anticipating Pink Floyd's sixth studio album – when the group's all-rounder (he was after all guitarist, vocalist, composer and producer) considered the merits of one of the world's best selling albums.

Sitting in a pub around the corner from the band's very own Britannia Row studios, he said, 'I think it's the least spontaneous of our albums, certainly less than any other of the ones we had done up until then.' Confirming that there were changes that came about as the band toured and played the songs live throughout 1972, he reflected on the time spent in the studio and how things progressed.

'The recording time was probably no more than six weeks and it never struck me as being a particularly difficult album but there was a lot of hard work put into it – rehearsing and writing it, formulating it and taking it out on the road.'

During my long stint at EMI (over 15 years), I came across the members of Pink Floyd either backstage after a show or on the odd occasion they would turn up for a meeting, but more often when EMI and Pink Floyd faced each other on the cricket field. We each had our own teams and the games, played seriously in regulation all-white gear and at corporate and village sports grounds became an annual sporting fixture for a few years.

I recall that the only rule we had about competing with one of our best selling acts was that, when taking on umpiring duties, we would be guided by the state of contract negotiations – if they had recently re-signed then all questionable decisions went against them, but if a new contract was in the offing, then they were given more than the benefit of the doubt when it came an appeal for leg before wicket or a catch behind.

In 1988 Gilmour and I chatted again, this time at Abbey Road studios, and once again the subject of Dark Side came up. 'It started off with a few pieces of music, then Roger came up with the ideas of what he wanted to make it all about,' he told me across a mixing console in one of the control rooms. While admitting that he couldn't remember very much about the actual recording sessions, he talked in an almost casual fashion about how one of the most influential and inspirational albums came to be. 'We carried on with him bringing in musical ideas and lyrical ideas and we all worked on it until it began to mean something. Then we came to Abbey Road and started knocking all the bits down.'

In 2012, 24 years after my last chat with Gilmour, I spoke about the album with the founder of the Smashing Pumpkins Billy Corgan, a man who is equally talented as a guitarist, singer, composer and producer. Although only five years old when *Dark Side of the Moon* came out – it was issued ten days before his sixth birthday – Corgan is by his own admission a big-time Floyd fan and something of a Dark Side expert.

Although Dark Side was not a record that he ever heard around his home, he did hear snatches of Floyd on Chicago's radio stations in the seventies and eighties – 'We had very progressive radio in Chicago and Floyd were a very big band in the city' he recalls. However, it was the band's 1979 album *The Wall* which properly alerted Corgan to the British four-piece. 'It was one of the first of their albums that I paid any attention to, and then *Wish You Were Here* was my get-me-through-my-grandmother-dying song.'

Working backwards from *The Wall* and *Wish You Were Here*, Corgan eventually hit on *Dark Side of the Moon*. 'My friends were saying 'You should listen to the whole album, really listen to it', and when I did hear it I was lucky because there was no mythology built up around it. I was aware of them in a general sense – I knew a few songs – but had no real knowledge of the Syd Barrett era for instance.'

However, once he got into the album Corgan admits he was hooked. '*Dark Side of the Moon* was probably the first time where I realised that there was this other level of organisation and I needed to pay attention to it. Then my relationship with them began to mature and I began to investigate everything.'

During my 30 minute phone call to him in his home town of Chicago, Corgan waxes lyrical about Dark Side and the impact it has had on him both as a fan and a musician. 'I very much believe it is a concept album and the fact that the cover has got nothing to do with the music is classic Floyd to me – how they took these simple things, put them together in a way that seems to have no synchronicity and amplify their meaning.'

'And it even works for their music,' he continued. 'In the band we call it 'the Pink Floyd breakdown', the very simple bass line and simple drum beat yet it sounds mystic and epic and like 'What is that?''.

By his own admission Corgan has 'spent a lot of time breaking down' Pink Floyd, and his assessment of the band member's skills and contributions confirms his fascination with their work. 'It is fascinating that David Gilmour's guitar playing in the beginning is pretty good but not remarkable, but I don't think any of them, probably including him, could have guessed that he would turn into a world-class guitar player. I was lucky enough that I got to talk to Dave and he told me that he learned a lot of his guitar chords from Syd Barrett.'

Turning his attention to the album's main creative force at that time Corgan says, 'Who knew that the insane architectural mind of Roger Waters would be able to go to other levels of concept beyond the vague? You look at *Ummagumma* and *Meddle* and you see flashes of it but it's not cohesive in the way of *Dark Side of the Moon*.'

While Corgan agrees with the suggestion that Dark Side would probably not have been made had Barrett remained with the band – 'Had Roger not been able to come forward they would not have made the album' – he is is most impressed how it all finally came to fruition. Noting that after Barrett's departure 'they really struggled and went from an A level psychedelic outfit to a meandering band with flashes of brilliance', he adds: 'What is fascinating to me about Pink Floyd is that they are a sum of the parts. And I actually like the parts very much but there's something about the sum of the parts which is mind-boggling. If you take Roger as a singer he is pretty tart, Gilmour is a little too sweet but that combo – there's something about that combo, the way they go back and forth – it's magical.'

Corgan's trawl through the complete works of Pink Floyd leads him to believe that 'you can learn more from *Dark Side of the Moon* by listening to their earlier albums than you can by listening to *Dark Side of the Moon* which is like the perfect film. You have to listen to the old albums to see them fumbling through things conceptually. You see flashes that were stitched into Dark Side later.'

Through his long and determined study of Floyd's musical efforts,

Corgan offers up the suggestion that the band's multi-million selling, record breaking album is 'emotional in a very weird way'. He continues, 'There's a real distance and austerity in the emotion which gives it that timeless, haunting quality. It's emotional but very measured and a lot of the songs are just two chords – it's very minimalistic anyway so why does it conjure up this tremendous emotion?'

Despite achieving global sales figures which run into many millions, the success of *Dark Side of the Moon* has intrigued people for years. 'Why, was it really that good?' are questions often asked and Corgan has his own theory. 'I didn't grow up in an English grove but it very much sums up the sense of suburban isolation. I would say that particularly in Chicago it really resonated with the working class out in the 'burbs more so than the city.

'Back then it was still very much a direct experience – you put on the album, put on your headphones and cranked up your stereo and it was immersive. And you had an hour in which to listen to it – imagine going an hour now without being interrupted or looking at your phone to see if you are going to be interrupted.'

He also views the band's lack of support for the album in the media as something else that was special to Floyd. 'They are a rare band where their modus operandi worked – I do like being difficult at times but it's probably worked against me more than for me, but somehow with them it works. They got more by doing less.'

Confirming his position as a true Floyd fan Corgan explains that he was quick to get hold of a copy of the *Dark Side of the Moon* box set, and that he was surprised by what he heard. 'I sat down to listen to it. I've got this $60,000 stereo and I'm trying to have a fresh experience and I was so surprised at how little was going on because in my mind it's this epic thing – I don't know how they do it.'

And the next move was for him to share his listening experience with the rest of his band. 'I said at band rehearsal – we talk about them a lot at practice because it's one of the models we try to learn from – 'How do you make something so simple so good?' and our guitar player said 'You just have to make the right choice,' and Floyd make the right choice. If it was tilted one way or another it could become schlock or schmaltz.'

Despite his enduring passion for Floyd, Corgan has performed very few of their songs during his live shows – there are versions of 'Lucifer Sam' and 'Set The Controls for the Heart of the Sun' – but at the Rock'n'Roll Hall of Fame awards show in 1996 he was not only invited to induct them but also to join them on stage in a version of 'Wish You Were Here', the song he turned to when his grandmother was dying.

In his speech in New York, Corgan described Pink Floyd as being 'everything that's great about rock – grandeur, pomposity, nihilism, humour and of course space' and *Dark Side of the Moon* as being 'the ultimate synthesis of sound and vision and lyrics – it stands as a great crowning achievement in music.'

Despite his love of the album, Corgan has always been reluctant to perform anything from *Dark Side of the Moon.* – 'We've never done anything on stage from Dark Side because I tend to avoid anything that's obvious' – but he ended our conversation in September 2012 by telling me that 'Breathe' was a song that is in his range. 'I could do a really nice version of that song and actually I am playing an acoustic set tomorrow night at a tea house locally and I think I'll play it in honor of our talk.'

(*Sadly it seems that, the next night, on September 13 2012, Corgan did not feature Breathe during either of his acoustic two shows at the opening of his new teahouse Madame Zu Zu's.*)

Looking back on the album years after its release, the members of Pink Floyd could contribute very little to explain its enormous worldwide success. 'It must have captured a spirit of that moment or something … but to be honest I don't really understand why it did quite as well as it did,' said Dave Gilmour while Rick Wright concluded, 'It touched a nerve. It seemed like everyone was waiting for this album, for someone to make it.'

According to Nick Mason, 'Something came together but there's no way that this record is stunningly better than the great albums of the last two decades', while Roger Waters, the main creative force behind the album, suggested, 'I think its enduring appeal comes from a combination of different factors. It is very listenable … There are lots of things on it that you recognise' and he concluded by saying, 'Although it wasn't the first of its kind in terms of the concept record idea, maybe it was the first one that had a heart.'

That's what they said near the end of the 1990s but when asked to comment, contribute or support this particular project to honour 40 years of *Dark Side of the Moon*, the surviving three members of Pink Floyd were less than enthusiastic. Representatives for Mason told me, 'The band have their own plans with regard to the 40th anniversary of *Dark Side of the Moon*. Consequently Nick does not wish to participate in the proposed book', while the management office of Waters thanked me for requesting his involvement and support towards 'a 40th Anniversary Book of the release of Pink Floyd's The *Dark Side of the Moon*' before adding 'his consent is not given.'

At the same time, the reply on behalf of Gilmour explained that 'David (never Dave) will be unlikely to want to be interviewed about the 40th anniversary' and later added 'he's always been circumspect on 'birthdays' for albums.' In the light of that reply, it seems that Mason's anniversary plans might not get Gilmour's full backing either.

It's perhaps interesting to note that the replies representing Mason, Waters and Gilmour titled the album slightly differently. In the note from Mason's office it was *Dark Side of the Moon* while Waters' representatives opted for *The Dark Side of the Moon*. And while you might question whether it actually matters as to what it was called officially, there are a few interesting contradictions along the way.

Harvest label manager at the time Nick Mobbs has no doubts and cites his original 1973 blue label pressing of the album with the title *The Dark Side of the Moon* printed across it. While he says, 'My feeling is that the correct title is 'The Dark Side' and label copy was always very carefully compiled and checked', he also adds a fascinating possible explanation for the title. 'There again, it could have been as random as me ringing their manager Steve O'Rourke to query the title. And I can just imagine him answering 'Oh let's go with 'the' – I'll make an executive decision'.'

However the man charged with designing the cover, the label and all the advertisements that went with the album is far from convinced about the word 'The'. Aubrey 'Po' Powell, co-founder of Hipgnosis, says, 'As far as I was concerned it was always just *Dark Side of the Moon* and I have never heard it referred to as The Dark Side', which is odd as the original record label in 1973 included the word 'The'.

Despite those two contrasting testaments from men who were involved in the creation and release of the album, it's relevant to note that EMI, parent company of the Harvest label, were at least consistent back in 1973. All the press adverts – designed by Hipgnosis – have the title as The Dark Side as did the 30th anniversary edition from 2003, and the various re-releases in 2011: the six-disc Collectors set, the re-mastered CD and the heavyweight vinyl version. But there are two little inconsistencies from the EMI vaults.

The original CD release in 1985 has the title printed across the disc and down the spine as simply *Dark Side of the Moon* while the reproduction sticker on the cover goes for The Dark Side and the company's comprehensive Harvest label tribute box set entitled *Harvest Festival* also lists it as simply Dark Side. And in author Peter Martland's official history of EMI The First 100 Years he too goes for just Dark Side. At the same EMI's sister company in America, Capitol Records, were the height of consistency with ALL their adverts, press releases and printed references to the album coming down firmly in favour of The Dark Side.

And that still leaves us with an assortment of newspapers, magazines, books and chart listings which have, over the years, come down on one side or the other mainly through a combination of familiarity, conjecture and contradictions.

Those who go for *The Dark Side of the Moon* include Wikipedia; The Guinness Book of Hit Singles and Albums; Billboard Book of Number One Albums; Billboard Book of Top 40 Albums; Rolling Stone magazine; Guinness Book of Rock Stars; The Great Rock Discography; authors Clive Davis, John Harris, Glenn Povey and band member Nick Mason; plus charts in Sounds, Billboard, Music Week, Melody Maker and New Musical Express.

In the list of those who opt for no definite article and settle on just *Dark Side of the Moon* are critics' reviews in NME, MM and Sounds; news stories in NME and MM; Billboard's Top 200 album chart (although they have also used the word 'The' on occasions); Rough Guide To Pink Floyd; Mojo's 1998 special; Penguin Encyclopedia of Pop Music; Rock Chronicles; The Complete Guide to Pink Floyd; Faber Companion to 20th Century Popular Music; Guinness Rockopedia; EMI's The Incredible Music Machine story; and authors Mark Blake … and Nick Mason (again!)

And the only and obvious question about these 'The' or 'not to The' alternatives is 'does it really matter what the album is called?' and the answer is, of course, probably not. At the end of the day it was and still is the music that mattered to those who bought the album, reviewed it, listed it or wrote about it – and made it. As a matter of interest I have referred to the album throughout this book (other than in direct quotes) as *Dark Side of the Moon* or simply as Dark Side but that's just because, when I worked at EMI, that what we always called it and I guess I'm stuck with forever thinking of it in those terms – or words.

Whatever it was called, all the 'bits they knocked down in the studio' according to Gilmour, eventually became a collection of tracks which have been generally accepted as the first progressive rock concept album and a work, which according to an Australian survey, is the best record to have to sex to. But it is more than that – more even than British Prime Minister David Cameron's favourite record according to a 2012 poll of Great British Music … where, incidentally, it was listed as The *Dark Side of the Moon*.

It has been variously described over the years by writers and publications as: 'A masterpiece to condense all your earthly woes into 43 cosmic minutes' (Mojo); 'A tuneful, rousing set of brilliant songs. For Floyd virgins this is the place to start' (1001 Albums You Must Hear Before You Die); 'A masterpiece … a meticulous concept … regarded by many as the greatest album of all time' (The Great Rock Discography); and 'One of the great monuments of rock history – as overwhelmingly aesthetically as it is statistically' (Phil Sutcliffe). In Q magazine's poll of the top 50 albums of the 1970s, where it was placed second behind The Clash's London Calling, Dark Side was described as '… an album which combined underlying quietness, discipline and restraint with eruptions of unbridled emotion. Such dynamics of sound and emotion have rarely been matched.'

A host of polls run by magazines, radio and TV stations have also seen the album firmly logged into most Greatest Albums of All-time listings – Planet Rock listeners voted it the 'greatest of all time' while listeners to the Australian Broadcasting Corporation named it their 'favourite album'. It was number two in America's National Association of Recording Merchandisers 'Definitive 200' poll and eighth in New

Musical Express's 2006 poll for 'best album of all-time'.

And along the way the landmark cover artwork has also been proclaimed as the 'greatest of all-time' by rock website Music. Radar, second in Rolling Stone's list of best album covers and as the fourth 'greatest in history' by VH1's audience. For co-designer Po Powell the runner-up awards come as no surprise. 'In the polls of album covers Peter Blake (designer of Sgt Pepper) is always number one of course, unfortunately, but *Dark Side of the Moon* is usually in the top three.'

While he may sometimes rue the work by Blake on The Beatles' 1967 album release, Powell is still quick to acknowledge the influence of that work on the aspiring young designers of the day. 'The defining moment in album cover design was Sgt Pepper … artists started to insist on controlling their own creative work including their image and albums covers were part of that,' he says.

Since 1979 when Dark Side was first re-mastered and re-released there has been an almost continuous flow of 'new' versions including its debut in 1985 as a Compact Disc, the 1988 'Ultradisc' gold CD, its re-issue in 1992 as part of a *Shine On* box set and a year later its re-appearance as part of the 20th anniversary box set. An updated quadraphonic 30th anniversary version was then issued in 2003 followed by another version in 2007 to celebrate 40 years of the most familiar and famous Pink Floyd line-up, established after Barrett's departure..

The ultimate 2011 six-disc box set Why Pink Floyd? included engineer and producer Alan Parsons' original quad mixes plus some early alternate mixes he worked on 'after hours' in Abbey Road studios in 1972 and 1973 at the time of the original Dark Side sessions. The fact that they were included without anyone asking or telling Parsons – and he acknowledges that, as they are the property of EMI and as he was a staff engineer assigned to work with Floyd at the time, perhaps nobody actually needed his permission – was further aggravated by the band's thoughtlessness. 'They've haven't seen fit to send me a copy and that has been the situation for the last 40 years when I have asked to be recognised for my part in The *Dark Side of the Moon*. Both the band and the record company have failed to give me any recognition.'

And, perhaps in the light of this situation, Parsons occasionally reflects on the situation that exists between himself and the band who, while they didn't launch his career, did play a major part in establishing his reputation. 'There wasn't an acrimonious split with the band at the time, the acrimony has only started recently,' he confirms.

Despite its highly personalised lyrics and its presentation as a concept album – plus the lack of major hit singles – the music on Dark Side has been covered by a surprising array of artists. While nowhere near the thousands who have attempted songs such as Paul McCartney's 'Yesterday' or George Harrison's 'Something', the whole album rather than any individual tracks has been given a new – and often bizarre – lease of life by an interesting collection of musicians.

The Squirrels produced *The Not So Bright Side Of The Moon* in 2000 while Easy Star All Stars issued *Dub Side Of the Moon* in 2003. A complete a cappella version came from Voices On the Dark Side and Poor Man's Whiskey manufactured a bluegrass version entitled *Dark Side of the Moonshine*. In 2004 there was a complete string version and in 2004 *Return To The Dark Side of the Moon* featured prog rock acts such as Tommy Shaw, Dweezil Zappa and Rick Wakeman. Finally, in 2009 psychedelic rock band The Flaming Lips, together with fellow Oklahoma band Stardeath & White Dwarfs, issued a complete re-make of Dark Side with guest players Henry Rollins and Peaches.

So while Dark Side has topped a few of the best ever album

polls, and its cover has won similar accolades, the real impressive reading comes when we flick through the sales and chart statistics for the genuine article. As of April 2013 *Dark Side of the Moon* (with or without 'The') had appeared in Billboard's Top 200 album chart for a total of 829 weeks and been on the magazine's Catalogue Charts every week since they began in 1991.which adds to a combined total of 1994 weeks .... or more than 38 years

In fact on its first outing in the US charts it clocked up a grand total of 741 consecutive weeks on the chart between March 1973 and July 1988 – that's over 14 years without a break. It was during this run that Dark Side overtook Johnny Mathis's 1958 Greatest Hits album as the album with most weeks on the US chart. September 29 1983 saw it hit 491 weeks and pass the record set by Mathis in 1968. Dark Side went on to pass 500 weeks in January 1984, 600 weeks in November 1985 and 740 weeks in June 1988.

The album's extraordinary chart success in America, with new records being broken year after year, made an impression on Waters who commented, 'What's interesting, I think, is the fact that we will always be remembered for the number of weeks *Dark Side of the Moon* remained on the Billboard charts and not for anything we did.' In a way perhaps he was right but In 2013 the US Library of Congress acknowledged more than just the chart success of *Dark Side of the Moon* when they announced that the album Is to be preserved as part of the National Record Registry whichh honours song and sounds whichh are "culturally, historically and aesthetically important and/or inform or reflect life in the United States."

As the album was released in 1973 and the US cut-off date for album sales certification was January 1976, Dark Side had to wait until 1990 to be certified 15 times platinum for 15 million sales in America. Meanwhile in the UK, it had an unbroken run of 310 weeks in the chart from its day of release in March 1973, and by April 2013 it had notched up a total of 609 weeks on the chart. Although its last appearance in the UK top ten was in February 1975, the album was recognised as a gold album in Music Week's May 31 1975 chart thanks to sales worth £250,000.

A week later it had jumped to unofficial platinum status with sales worth £1 million and appeared in a Top 30 chart alongside fellow platinum albums The Singles by The Carpenters and Elton John's Greatest Hits. Finally, seven months later, on January 1 1976 – when the first official sales awards were introduced by the British Phonographic Industry – it was officially certified as a platinum album for sales of 300,000, one of just 14 albums to be recognised in that first year of BPI certifications.

After the UK and US had recognised the album's achievements, the rest of the world began to log sales of Dark Side and it has now been certified as platinum in France, Italy and Poland; double platinum in Argentina, Austria and Germany; double diamond in Canada and a massive 14 times platinum in Australia.

Together those awards add up to sales of around 4 million while a host of other countries will have contributed their bit to the Dark Side pot. In the UK total sales stand at a further 4 million – it is the eight best selling album of all-time (Queen's Greatest Hits leads the pack on 5.8 million), while America still lists it at 15 million copies.

While worldwide sales for any album are rarely going to be either confirmed or authenticated by artists or their record companies, the consensus of opinion is that *Dark Side of the Moon* has a definite placing in the top ten list of best selling albums of all-time. The estimates and guesstimates put the total sales figure at anywhere between 35 and 43 million copies, which means it is up there alongside Their Greatest Hits *1971-1975* by The Eagles, Rumours by Fleetwood Mac, AC/DC's Back In Black and Bat Out Of Hell from Meat Loaf. All these are in the mix for a top five place behind the unopposed all time best seller – Michael Jackson's Thriller which on a good day has been credited with sales of 110 million. It's all the more amazing to think that before Dark Side no album by Pink Floyd – including their UK number one hit *Atom Heart Mother* (1970) – had sold over 250,000 copies.

While we may not have a totally accurate sales figure for *Dark Side of the Moon* we can take comfort from a claim made back in 1998 that it was still reckoned to be selling a million copies a year, and that just seven years ago (in 2005) 8,000 copies were still reportedly flying out of US record shops each week.

At the same time it was estimated that one in every five households in the UK owned a copy of the album while somebody else calculated that one in 14 people in America under the age of 50 owns or has owned a copy. And this book is dedicated to all those people (over or under 50) who have the album in their collection … and for those who have not yet realised what they are missing – even 40 years on.

Brian Southall

For Kelly, Rich and Alyssa – shine on!

DARK SIDE OF THE MOON REVEALED

Chapter One

'In 1965 Barrett and Waters met an experimental percussionist and an extraordinarily gifted keyboards player – Nick Mason and Rick Wright respectively. The result was Pink Floyd.' In this brief sentence, running to a few more than 20 words, the official Pink Floyd website records how the band, which was at the forefront of the new movement that helped take British music out of swinging sixties pop and into a new era of hip psychedelia, started out.

Of course there is more to the story than those few words. First there is the fact that bass player Roger Waters first met Mason and Wright when they all studied at London's Regent Street Polytechnic and even helped form a band called Sigma 6 with Clive Metcalfe, Keith Noble and the latter's sister Sheila.

That was early in 1964 and within months the band had been re-named The Abdabs (although they were occasionally called the Architectural Abdabs and even the Screaming Abdabs) and recruited a new guitarist Bob Klose and a singer – an air force dental assistant named Chris Dennis – as Metcalfe and both Keith and Sheila Noble departed. Another change of name saw the new line-up christened The Tea Set and soon after Syd Barrett arrived on the scene.

A school friend of Roger's from Cambridge, where Waters' mother had also taught him at junior school, Barrett eventually took over as frontman of the Tea Set when Dennis left for an RAF posting overseas. The five-piece of Mason, Waters and Wright plus Klose and Barrett took to performing as the Regent Street Poly's house band with a set list featuring the current R&B favourites and acting as support to the main act.

In the very last month of 1964, the Tea Set managed to get their first-ever studio session, utilizing some free time thanks to a friend of Wright who worked in the studio. They recorded four tracks, including the blues classic 'I'm A King Bee' and three songs written by Barrett, and followed up this new adventure by landing a residency at the Countdown Club, located just off fashionable Kensington High Street, in early 1965. In a further attempt to find fame and fortune, the Tea Set entered two talent contests – one run by the Country Club in North London and another organised by the leading music paper Melody Maker.

When the final of the Country Club contest clashed with a heat in MM's Beat Contest, the band managed to find a way to appear in both competitions but after losing out in the MM show, they were then disqualified from the Country Club event for turning up late. Following the departure of Klose, the group worked their way through 1965 happy to be known as the Tea Set until they discovered there was another band with the same name. Within days Barrett had solved the problem by coming up with the name The Pink Floyd Sound, in honour of two American bluesmen Pink Anderson and Floyd Council.

According to early band member Chris Dennis, speaking in 2012, the name change came about as the band prepared for a gig at a private party in Surrey. 'At that time we didn't even have a name' says the man who was eventually replaced by Barrett. 'We were rehearsing blues songs for our first gig. On the night Syd ran through and said, 'I've got a name – it's going to be called Pink Floyd. I didn't like it at the time because it didn't make sense.'

Under their new name, Pink Floyd Sound stepped away from London in October 1965 to play at the 21st birthday party for up and coming designer Storm Thorgerson's girlfriend Libby and her twin sister Rosie. Held in Cambridge, the gig's support acts were a young folk singer named Paul Simon and a band called Jokers Wild who featured a local Cambridge lad named David Gilmour on guitar.

The relationship between the members of Pink Floyd Sound and Thorgerson and his business partner-to-be Aubrey Powell began back in the days before they had even signed a record deal. 'We were all buddies back then', says Powell. 'Our relationship with Floyd was always very amicable and full of banter and we were all bright and well educated … and very opinionated.'

'Storm and Roger always had an intellectual tussle about things which was very healthy', adds Powell, and he goes on to explain that Barrett was at the heart of the relationship between the designers and the musicians. 'Syd was the common theme – Storm and I shared a flat with him in London and he and Dave were very close at college and they shared guitar licks. It was all very incestuous.'

Later this early friendship would turn into a fully fledged business arrangement but in early 1966 they focused their attention on another opportunity in one of London's most famous rock clubs. In March 1964, the Marquee had moved from its original site in Oxford Street to Wardour Street in the heart of Soho and become famous as the venue that opened every night of the week and regularly offered up The Who, Manfred Mann, The Move and Cream amongst others.

Up until 1966 nothing happened at The Marquee on Sunday afternoons but then an American named Steve Stollman started up a 'psychedelic grove' called 'Spontaneous Underground' which featured musicians, poets and artists. Floyd turned up — alongside aspiring folk singer Donovan – and began to gain some attention as they slowly dropped their blues repertoire in favour of what was described as 'extended psychedelic music'.

Amongst the audience at one of these shows were Peter Jenner and Andrew King who ran their own record label DNA. On the lookout for a pop band for the label, Jenner recalls seeing Floyd and hearing some 'weird and strange' sounds emerging from one of their Sunday afternoon sessions. 'That was the thing that got me. This was avant-garde!' he says while also noting, 'I did think the 'Sound' part of their name was pretty lame.'

While Floyd were not keen to sign to the DNA label, they were in need of some expert guidance and responded to Jenner's persistence by agreeing that the two young graduates – Jenner from Cambridge and King from Oxford – could manage the band that would very soon be known simply as Pink Floyd. In an unusual arrangement, Jenner and King decided that the four members should become partners in their Blackhill Enterprises company. All six of the partners would own an equal share of the business which was now primed to focus all its attention on the Floyd, although later acts such as Roy Harper, Edgar Broughton and Marc Bolan would also join the ranks.

Very soon Pink Floyd became regulars on London's growing underground scene, playing at the All Saints Hall in West London's Notting Hill district through October and November 1966. According to Melody Maker's Nick Jones, who saw one of their early shows, 'the group's space sounds promised very interesting things to come' while he concluded, 'The Floyd need to write more of their material ... if they can incorporate their electronic prowess with some melodic and lyrical songs, getting away from dated R&B things, they could well score in the near future.'

At a show described as a 'pop/op/costume/masque/fantasy-loon/blow out/drag ball', Floyd joined forces with Soft Machine to provide the music for a party in Chalk Farm's Roundhouse theatre to celebrate the launch of the IT (International Times) newspaper. Other Roundhouse shows saw Floyd on the bill with the likes of Geno Washington, the Alan Bown Set, Cream, The Who and The Move. And two months after his October review, MM's Jones now reckoned that Pink Floyd – by December 31 1966 – had a 'promising sound and some very groovy picture slides which attract more attention than the group'.

Another new and interested party was booking agent Bryan Morrison who had heard good things about Pink Floyd – and had even booked them without ever seeing them live – and he then made it his business to turn up at a rehearsal as they ran through their likely first single, 'Arnold Layne'.

The man in charge of the session was American producer Joe Boyd who arrived in the UK in late 1965 to work for the US label Elektra but soon found himself embroiled in London's growing underground scene. His enthusiasm eventually led to him opening the UFO Club in the basement of an Irish dance hall called the Blarney Club on London's Tottenham Court Road. Pink Floyd were on the bill at the club's opening night on December 23 1966.

Having booked Floyd for his club, Boyd then found himself involved in trying to get the band their first record deal and his first contact was with the German label Polydor which was keen to break into the UK record market. They liked what they heard on the demo tapes made by Boyd and the discussions centred around a deal to sign Pink Floyd to the label via Boyd's Witchseason

Productions.

However when Morrison saw the contract he had some misgivings and proposed a new idea – his company would fund the first recordings by the band and then try and sell them to either EMI or Decca, the two giant British record companies. The next idea was for Boyd to produce both 'Arnold Layne' and the B-side 'Candy and a Currant Bun', but as an employee of Floyd. He eventually agreed but on the condition that he also produced the group's first album, something Morrison doubted would happen, as he knew that the two major companies both preferred to use one of their own in-house producers.

On January 11 1967 Pink Floyd and Joe Boyd went into the Sound Techniques Studio close to Chelsea's Kings Road to record the band's proposed first single which Boyd recalls as being 'tricky' with only four-track machines available. 'In 1967 mixes were like recording takes; you had to get it in one pass or go back to the top and start again,' he recounted before confirming that 'we all felt good about the results.'

Armed with the tracks Morrison went to EMI who also liked what they heard and offered £5,000 to sign Floyd – who needed the cash to buy a new van – but, just as Morrison had predicted, they wanted the band to use the company's Abbey Road Studios and one of EMI's staff producers. While Jenner, King and the band felt some guilt about deserting Boyd, Mason explained that 'you did not sign with the company [EMI] and then bring along your pet producer.'

But even though the deal with EMI had been signed, the band still had to play an 'artist test' audition which was compulsory for all new signings – even one who had brought a ready-to-go first single with them. And although EMI did attempt a re-recording, it was Boyd's original version which was issued in March 1967.

Two months before the release of 'Arnold Layne', Melody Maker carried a feature under the headline 'Who's Psychedelic Now?'

which threw a spotlight on The Move and Pink Floyd as leading purveyors of the new 'experimentation in light and sound'. While the paper were impressed with Floyd's progress from unknowns to a residency at the Marquee Club in just a matter of weeks, the band's drummer was seemingly less enthused with how they were being tagged. 'You have to be careful when you start on this psychedelic thing' said Mason. 'We don't call ourselves a psychedelic group. It's just that people associate us with this … it's something that has taken place all around us – not within us.'

And bass player Waters gave his reason for how the group were being labelled. 'I think the reason is that we've been employed by so many of these freak-out merchants. I sometimes think that it's only because we have lots of equipment and lighting and it saves the promoters from having to hire lighting.'

With the release of 'Arnold Layne' in March 1967, came the first music paper reviews of a Pink Floyd recording and MM's reviewer announced, 'It was interesting to see how the Floyd would fare with having to make a commercial single, but with their animated, almost electronic sound, which occasionally takes an unprecedented twist, they've made a good single.' In the same paper, Scott Walker, from The Walker Brothers, was assessing the singles in its Blind Date column and he pronounced as follows, 'It's grand. I like it. I have no idea who it is but I like it and I'm a good judge of things. It's different and the lyrics are interesting. It's about a transvestite? I haven't tried transvestism, yet.'

Thanks in part to this double thumbs-up from MM and the support of the BBC, 'Arnold Layne' made progress in the UK charts despite pirate station Radio London banning it because of its content and it eventually peaked at number 20. However, despite being filmed for *Top of the Pops*, Floyd did not get to feature on the show as the record slipped down the chart in the week they were set to be appear. Around the same time Floyd got the nod from another famous person when Paul McCartney, in Abbey Road studios recording Sgt Pepper's Lonely Hearts Club Band with The Beatles, told the press that he heard some of the tracks destined for the first Pink Floyd album and declared them 'knockout'.

Talking to MM in April 1967, Syd Barrett explained his thoughts behind the band's first hit. 'I thought 'Arnold Layne' was a nice name', he said before adding, 'Then I thought, 'Arnold must have a hobby' and it went from there. Arnold Layne just happens to dig dressing up in women's clothing. A lot of people do.' In the same article Rick Wright said, 'I think the record was banned not because of the lyrics but because they're against us as a group and against what we stand for' and it was left to Nick Mason to explain where Floyd fitted into music in Britain in 1967. 'We would like to think that we're the part of the creative half in that we write our own material and don't just record other people's numbers.'

As Floyd grew in popularity so they were booked into bigger and better venues and tours. They ended their run of 15 appearances at The Marquee (not including the early Sunday afternoon spots) in March 1967 and almost immediately went on to a '14 Hour Technicolour Dream' concert in April at Alexandra Palace. This was followed in May by a show at London's newly opened Queen Elizabeth Hall, plus a spot on Barbecue 67 in Spalding alongside Geno Washington and Jimi Hendrix.

These demands – and their increasing popularity - made it hard for them to continue with their dates at Joe Boyd's UFO Club where they had become regulars despite the producer-cum-club owner losing out on producing their records. But while the band argued that playing in Central London for £50 was no longer practical, Boyd was concerned that upping their fee would mean increasing the 10/- admission price. Eventually a compromise was reached and the bands agreed to play two shows for £75 each and a further one in June 1967 before the Floyd ended their association with the UFO in early September. By the time the club finally closed its doors on September 29 1967 – with Jeff Beck and Ten Years After on the bill – Floyd had notched up a total of ten UFO appearances.

Chapter Two

The follow-up to the hit 'Arnold Layne' was another Syd Barrett song called 'See Emily Play' and for this record the band made their debut on *Top of the Pops* on July 6 1967 around the same time as stalwart BBC disc jockey Pete Murray described the band as 'a con' on the popular Saturday night television panel show Juke Box Jury. Despite this assessment, NME's Derek Johnson was moved to declare that the single was 'crammed with weird oscillations, reverberations, electronic vibrations and fuzzy rumblings' before declaring, 'Should register.'

After Scott Walker's Blind Date review of the first release, it was Procol Harum leader Gary Brooker's turn to review Floyd's follow up single. 'The Pink Floyd. I can tell by the horrible organ sound. It's much better than 'Arnold Layne'. Much better. They are the only people doing this kind of scene and they have a very distinctive sound. What the hell is a psychedelic record anyway? Is it something with weird sounds on it?'

'See Emily Play' took Floyd into the UK top ten for the first time, peaking at number six ahead of the band being booked for an all-night 'Love In Festival' at Alexandra Palace on July 29/30 – tickets £1 – and the 7th National Jazz Pop Ballads & Blues festival at Royal Windsor racecourse on August 12, where tickets cost 15/-.

One of the last reviews of Floyd at the UFO came from MM's Roger Simpson who dubbed Floyd 'Britain's top psychedelic group' before suggesting that Floyd 'prefer playing the UFO-type audiences rather than provincial ones'. Talking to the music paper around the same time, Roger Waters confirmed that the band were having problems with their live dates. 'We're being frustrated at the moment by the fact that to stay alive we have to play lots and lots of places and venues that are not really suitable. That can't last obviously and we are happy to create our own venues.'

After suggesting that Floyd might even get a huge tent and take to the road like a travelling circus, the bass player explained, 'What we've got to do now is get together a stage act that has nothing to do with our records.'

In August 1967 Pink Floyd issued their debut album *Piper at the Gates of Dawn* on EMI's Columbia label, and saw it move into the UK top ten, climbing to number six in the chart during The Beatles 23-week reign at number one with *Sgt Pepper's Lonely Hearts Club Band*. The producer of Floyd's debut album was Norman Smith, the man assigned by EMI to produce the band after Joe Boyd. Smith, who worked as engineer on The Beatles' very first session at Abbey Road in 1962, had seen Floyd at the UFO Club and he was confident things would happen when they got into the studio. 'What I saw absolutely amazed me. I was still into creating and developing new electronic sounds in the control room and Pink Floyd, I could see, were into exactly the same thing. It was perfect marriage.'

On the back of Floyd's one and only appearance (on October 1 1967) as part of the Sunday At The Saville shows started by Beatles' manager Brian Epstein, the band travelled to the US in

October for their debut tour but by now everybody realised that drugs were beginning to take their toll on Syd Barrett. In August the band's first ever MM front page story – under the banner headline 'Pink Floyd Flake Out' – announced the cancellation of various dates, at a reported cost of £4,000, because Barrett was suffering from 'nervous exhaustion' . When they reached America two months later the guitarist refused to lip synch to 'Arnold Layne' on American Bandstand, and adopted a blank stare when asked questions.

After their third single 'Apples and Oranges' had failed to chart, Floyd joined a major UK package with Jimi Hendrix and The Move throughout November and into December 1967 but as Barrett became less dependable, the band were forced to bring in a deputy guitarist (The Nice's David O'List) for the shows that Barrett missed. And after the band had deliberately not picked up Barrett for a gig in Southampton in early 1968, they recruited Cambridge guitarist David Gilmour for their live shows.

According to Waters things were 'fine for a while … Syd even did a couple of gigs', but it wasn't a situation that was going to last. 'He was becoming crazier and crazier', explained Waters. 'I remember the final straw and that was when Syd suddenly decided that the answer to the band's problems was to introduce two saxophones and a girl singer.'

In January 1968 the pop world was told that Pink Floyd had grown to a five-piece as 'David Gilmur' (MM's spelling in their news story) had joined the band and would travel with them for their February European tour. Three months later came the news that everyone was expecting as Barrett finally split from the group he had founded and named three years earlier. The official line was that Barrett had left the group to 'concentrate on songwriting' and that Gilmour would feature on the band's next single 'It Would Be So Nice', released in April 1968.

In the months immediately after Barrett's departure, Floyd were reported to have introduced an 'azimuth coordinator' – providing an improved version of quadraphonic sound – into their live shows which included gigs at Covent Garden's Middle Earth club (members 16/- and guests 26/-) and the first ever free Hyde Park concert on June 29 supported by Jethro Tull, Roy Harper and a new act known as Tyrannosaurus Rex.

As the band returned to America for an 18-date tour, their second album *A Saucerful of Secrets*, produced by Smith at Abbey Road and featuring Barrett on one track, was released, and was greeted by a review in the August 3 issue of Melody Maker which said, 'Exciting, penetrating, experimental sounds by Britain's top psychedelic group much maligned and much misunderstood. They really score in recording rather than live performances ...' The cover artwork signalled the start of the band's partnership with the design team of Powell and Thorgerson at Hipgnosis, and this first effort drew on a combination of images from Marvel comics and the solar system.

The album, without Barrett's input and influence, represented a new direction for Floyd with Waters recalling, 'Syd moving out meant that we just had to start writing. In fact his leaving made us pursue the idea of the extended epic ... A Saucerful of Secrets was fifteen minutes or so long and that was considered rather outlandish at the time.'

The group ended 1968 with the release of their fifth single – 'Point Me at the Sky' – which signalled the end of their interest in the pop charts. Echoing the words of Rolling Stone Bill Wyman – 'We were all in bands making albums, no longer groups making singles' – Floyd focused their attention on a new album which would be a double set with one record as a live recording and the other disc featuring songs from the four members of the band. Pink Floyd was also in the process of being shifted from EMI's Columbia label to a new division set up to handle what was generally known as 'progressive music'. The name of this new label was Harvest.

According to original label manager Malcolm Jones, while Harvest acts had very little in common musically, their records, he reckoned 'are bought by the same section of the record buying public'. In an official EMI statement the initial Harvest releases would come from Edgar Broughton and Michael Chapman followed by Deep Purple, Pete Brown's Battered Ornaments and Shirley & Dolly Collins. It went on to say, 'Other acts scheduled for Harvest are Pink Floyd, Third Ear Band, Syd Barrett and the Pretty Things.' Melody Maker's response to the news was to ask, 'What's a company like EMI doing starting an underground label?'

On the back of two hit singles and their first two album releases Pink Floyd took sixth place in MM's 1969 Readers Poll for Best British Group - one place behind Cream and three ahead of The Who with The Beatles at number one – and the release of the double album *Ummagumma* in October 1969 took them to a new high of number five in the UK charts. Appearing in a list of Highly Recommended albums alongside releases from Cream, King Crimson, The Kinks, Pentangle and Soft Machine, the new Floyd release saw Melody Maker report, 'At last! Unutterably superb space music which will take your mind away out of the solar system and into another dimension altogether.'

Tasting chart success for the first time *Ummagumma*, produced by the band and Norman Smith, reached number 74 in the first month of 1970. Once again Hipgnosis produced an eye catching sleeve with a picture of the band in a house and garden with the same picture hanging on a wall in the house but with the four band members in different positions.

The new decade also saw Floyd earning much more money from their gigs than the meagre £15 they got for the International Times launch event, or even the £50 paid by the UFO Club. Amid stories that they charged £2,000 per concert, keyboard player Rick Wright explained that they would still appear for less. 'If a university can only fit 1,000 in the concert then we will only charge £400. Universities have put it around that we charge £1800 and they are frightened to approach is because they won't be able to afford the group.' And he went a stage further to admit, 'The money we live on comes from record royalties and the gig money is almost all spent on the upkeep of the band.'

Pink Floyd's fourth album in as many years came in the shape of *Atom Heart Mother* with its unique Hipgnosis designed cover photograph of a cow in a field. It was released in October 1970, ten months after the band had first presented the songs in Paris under the title 'The Amazing Pudding', and then again – as *Atom Heart Mother* – at the Bath Festival in June 1970. The band's first-ever UK number one hit, it peaked at #55 in the US but still heralded Floyd's arrival as a major international talent.

It was also the first album where the credits read 'produced by Pink Floyd, executive producer Norman Smith' and Gilmour once explained to me the reasons behind the change. 'Norman was the producer on all on our albums until he became listed as executive producer which was a neat way of saying that he didn't actually do anything.' The guitarist, however, went on to pay tribute to the man who, in 1971 and 1972, racked up three chart singles under the name Hurricane Smith which, in his own words brought him 'a lot stick about being a pop star' from the 'underground' acts he produced.

'He was wonderful and taught us lot about producing records,' was Gilmour's assessment of Smith who died in 2008. 'But it just came to the point where we had learnt enough from him, where he became redundant I suppose.'

In between making their own studio albums (and one live), Pink Floyd showed an increasing interest in films and soundtracks.

Starting in 1968, they supplied three versions of the 1967 song Interstellar Overdrive for the film *Tonite Let's All Make Love in London*, a semi documentary about life in swinging London in the sixties. In 1970 they were among an array of artists, including Roy Orbsion, The Grateful Dead and The Rolling Stones, who featured in Michaelangelo Antonioni's film *Zabriskie Point* which dealt with American counter culture. The follow up to the director's hit movie *Blow Up*, *Zabriskie Point* was a major commercial flop despite the inclusion of Floyd's 'Heart Beat Pig Meat', 'Come In Number 51 Your Time is Up' and 'Crumbling Land'.

In between they took a more pro-active role in Barbet Schroeder's 1969 film *More*, which told a story of heroin addiction in the island of Ibiza, by writing and performing the 13-track soundtrack and then releasing it as a Pink Floyd album in July 1969. Sandwiched between *A Saucerful of Secrets* and *Ummagumma*, it also reached the top ten in the UK.

Following Floyd's brief hold on the UK number one spot with *Atom Heart Mother* – they were number one for one week in between Simon and Garfunkel's *Bridge Over Troubled Water* and *Motown Chartbusters Vol 4* – the band's founding member Syd Barrett issued his second solo album in November 1970. Barrett followed his top 40 debut album *The Madcap Laughs* but with no promotion and no great support, it signaled the end of Barrett's recording career and he returned to Cambridge to live as a recluse.

However, his music lived on as part of the first Pink Floyd compilation album *Relics* which was surprisingly released on EMI's budget label Regal-Starline in April 1971. Three Barrett solo compositions – the hits 'Arnold Layne' and 'See Emily Play' plus 'Bike' – and the band's 'Interstellar Overdrive' were featured on this 11-track album which reached # 32 in the UK and #152 in America.

The band's schedule leading up to the release of their next

album included an appearance – as the only non-classical act on the bill – at the Montreux Music Festival in September 1971, where they performed *Atom Heart Mother*. This appearance, plus a US tour in October, led up to the release of *Meddle* which was announced in a Melody Maker news story on October 23 1971 which comprehensively reported, '*Meddle* the album comes in a double sleeve with a large blow up ear covered in drops of water and was produced by the group, and side two features one number, 'Echoes'.' It was in fact a pig's ear pictured underwater and said to represent the echoes featured on the album's major track.

The brief news item was followed soon after by a full page advert in all the music papers which featured four straightforward head and shoulder shots of the band members accompanied by just two lines of copy which said 'Pink Floyd * *Meddle*'. The new album was the first the band recorded away from Abbey Road studios where 16-track recording equipment had yet to be installed. Instead they worked on 16-track at AIR Studios, set high above London's Oxford Circus, with some extra work done at Morgan Sound and Abbey Road.

Meddle also represented a major shift in influence within the band as Barrett's legacy began to fade. 'From the early seventies on, I'd say, from *Meddle* on I made all the decisions', was how Waters viewed things within Pink Floyd as he apparently took on more responsibility including deciding, 'how often we're going to tour, how long the tours should be, which cities, when should our next record be, those kinds of things.'

While the new album failed to make it past #70 in America, it hit the number three spot in the UK in November 1971, trailing behind the chart-topping *Led Zeppelin 3*, and helped the band to pick up second place, behind Genesis, as Best British Group in MM's readers poll. However the same paper's writer Mick Watts was less than impressed with what he heard on Floyd's fifth studio album.

'One can't help but feel that Pink Floyd are so much sound and fury, signifying nothing. *Meddle* exhibits all their faults as well as their most successful points. Where there is little real musical substance to sustain those effects, how can the result be anything but a sound track to a non-existent movie?' He added, 'Listen to 'One of These Days', it's a throwback of 'Telstar' by The Tornados.'

On the other hand, Steve Peacock writing in Sounds showed no such doubts about the album as he wrote in November 1971, 'It's one of the most complete pieces of Pink Floyd music they've done. A very relaxed, very complete album from the Floyd and I think one that will keep revealing more of itself for a long time as you listen.'

At the outset of 1972, Pink Floyd already had on their minds the music that would transform their career and the listening habits of a generation, but there was still time to complete the soundtrack to another Barbet Schroeder film, *The Valley,* which follows the trail of a bunch of hippies as they trek through New Guinea.

Recorded in France's Château d'Hérouville studios near Paris, the album (called *Obscured by Clouds*) peaked at number six in the UK but took Floyd to new heights in America. Its entry in the Top 50 — at #46 – signalled a new wider acceptance of Pink Floyd which they would build on and successfully exploit over the next four decades ... beginning with their record-breaking next album..

DARK SIDE OF THE MOON REVEALED

Chapter Three

Sometime in the last week of March 1973, a young medical student called John rushed out to buy a copy of the new Pink Floyd album, *Dark Side of the Moon*. It had been officially released on Friday March 23 and John's rush to get to a record shop was prompted by the news that a new tax called VAT (Value Added Tax) was about to introduced. Records – both singles and albums – were included on the list of items to be taxed at the new 10% rate introduced by the Conservative government of Edward Heath.

Studying at Charing Cross Hospital and supported by a weekly allowance from his father of just £5, John was anxious to get the new album before the anticipated price increase came into force. However, what he didn't realise (and, it has to be said, neither did this author) was that the new tax levied on records would in fact result in a drop in prices.

Previously subject to Purchase Tax – which was banded at different levels dependant on the luxury status of goods and included records in the highest 25% bracket –- albums and singles would, after April 1 1973, be rated at just 10% under the new VAT system. This change meant that album prices dropped by somewhere around 10p or 12p and that John, had he waited a week, would have been able to buy the new Pink Floyd release at the new reduced Harvest label list price list of just £2.38p.

And something else that John didn't know was that the new album from Roger Waters, David Gilmour, Nick Mason and Rick Wright, which he was in such a hurry to buy, had taken them over 18 months to complete.

The first conversations about *Dark Side of the Moon* apparently took place between dates during the first half of 1971 on the UK leg of their scheduled global tour. By August of that year they were in Japan and Australia before spending September and October in Europe, and then the US leg of their *Meddle* tour with a string of dates throughout October and November.

If the exact date of these initial conversations is far from clear, the venue is in no doubt. The conversations regarding a follow-up album were held around drummer Nick Mason's kitchen table in St Augustine's Road, Camden, in North London. Here, Waters began to explain his idea for an album which, he said, 'might be about the pressures and preoccupations that divert us from our potential for positive action.'

Under the stewardship of bass player Waters, the band then began coming up with ideas for the new album which in later years they would each analyse and explain differently. According to guitarist Gilmour it was about 'the pressures of modern living and all the elements that one goes through that conspire to send some people insane', and drummer Mason agreed that it was about 'the pressures of modern life'. The band's keyboard player Wright saw it as being 'about the business, suffused with references to the life of a rock band.'

It is claimed that one of the earliest examples of Pink Floyd's new work in progress came in September 1971 when some say that a demo recording of a track called 'Money' was featured during the band's appearance on BBC Radio 1's *In Concert* series. Made in Waters' small studio in the garden of his house in New North Road in the north London district of Islington, this version of Money supposedly featured the sound of loose change being spun in a bowl on the potters' wheel normally used by Judy Waters to create her ceramics. However the show's producer Jeff Griffin has no recollection of it and suggests that it might just be 'one of those internet myths'.

By early 1972, however, *Dark Side of the Moon* had begun to take shape as the next instalment in the band's creative story, as they took their new songs on the road as part of their 14-date UK tour which opened at Brighton Dome on January 20. Unfortunately this first airing of music from their as yet un-started new album fell victim to some technical gremlins and was abandoned during their performance of 'Money' when Waters announced 'due to severe mechanical and electric horrors we can't do any more of that bit, so we'll do something else'.

In the audience that night was journalist Martin Hayman and his review in the music paper *Sounds* reflected the band's popularity. 'But this is the first performance of their new live show and a wildly cheering audience left them in no doubt as what they felt about it,' he wrote before adding, 'Problems forced them to abandon a new piece which they described as their masterpiece.'

Also on that tour was EMI special promotions man Martin Nelson who focused his attention on breaking just a handful of the company's acts in the south of England. 'The idea was to try and develop avant-garde music and we had Queen, Cockney Rebel and Floyd', recalls the man who actually joined EMI in the same month as Floyd went on tour.

Nelson's job was to load up his company estate car with posters, record sleeves and any other material relating to the band's catalogue and put up displays in record shops and in the foyer of each venue as the tour moved around the UK. One of the bonuses for Nelson was that he also saw every show on the tour. 'I had my own place at the side of the stage from where I watched them perform every night and the first half of the show was new material which would eventually become *Dark Side of the Moon.*'

While Nelson recalls that none of the band ever did interviews and rarely talked to anybody – 'all they were interested in was their music' – he does recall a day off that was spent on the south coast where they had played Brighton, Portsmouth, Bournemouth and Southampton on four consecutive nights before taking a break ahead of resuming the tour in Newcastle on January 27.

'I went off with them on days off and one of them was spent at a house owned by Nick Mason's parents somewhere near Brighton. It had a fantastic garden which led down to the sea and we had tea in the garden one afternoon and on other days we went to a country pub. They were always very affable and I really liked them,' he says.

As the tour meandered up and down Britain, the band got to grips with their new creation and eventually played the first complete live performance of *Dark Side of the Moon* at Portsmouth Guildhall on January 21 while dates in Plymouth and Manchester were cancelled or rescheduled. In mid-February, they ended the tour with four nights at London's Rainbow Theatre in Finsbury Park.

Prior to Floyd taking a set list comprising a collection of both old and new music on the road, the band had made the decision to return to EMI's Abbey Road studios to start to prepare the music for their new album. The legendary studio made famous by The Beatles throughout the sixties had been deemed out of date by Floyd when they recorded *Meddle*, as it persevered with 8-track recording techniques. But Abbey Road's switch in 1972 to the latest 16-track machines tempted the band back there, to the studio where they first cut records in 1967.

In fact preliminary work on the album had begun back in November 1971 at Decca's London studios and continued sporadically in Abbey Road during the first two months of 1972 as the band combined recording with dates on their UK tour.

By the Rainbow Theatre shows on 17–20 February, the new work they were offering was still being billed as '*Dark Side of the Moon – A Piece For Assorted Lunatics*' and the performances brought mixed reviews from the music press. Now an agricultural consultant for the BBC Radio 4 series The Archers, Steve Peacock was a staff writer for Sounds in 1972 and his concert review read as follows: '*Dark Side of the Moon* lasts an hour, is based around a theme of madness – whatever you understand by that – and takes you through a bewildering yet completely logical series of emotional changes. Musically it's inventive and well structured, lyrically it's strong and the uses of quadraphonic sound helps with a rare sense of total involvement.' And he went on to say, somewhat prophetically, 'Finally a plea: don't let *Dark Side of the Moon* become a millstone round their necks. Treat it with respect and it'll stay a living, classic musical creation.'

Less enthusiastic was Melody Maker's Chris Charlesworth who suggested, 'Musically there were some great ideas but the sound effects often left me wondering if I was in a bird cage at Regent's Park zoo. At times they were pretentious to the point of absolute silliness but I was obviously in a minority.' On the other hand that esteemed business newspaper the Financial Times chimed in to say that 'the Floyd have the furthest frontiers of pop music to themselves.'

One unplanned and significant outcome from their London shows was the release of a quality bootleg of their live *Dark Side of the Moon* performances. For some the album represented a permanent reminder of the show while other fans thought it was the official follow-up to *Meddle*. Either way it sold over 120,000 and put a permanent halt to Floyd's plans to feature an album's worth of unreleased material in their live concerts, as Gilmour confirmed in a 1994 interview. Explaining that the album's strength came from being played live before it was recorded, he said, 'You couldn't do that now of course, you'd be bootlegged out of existence.'

Nick Mobbs had been appointed as manager of EMI's Harvest label in 1971 and he arrived at the company as a devoted Pink Floyd fan. 'I think they welcomed my arrival as I don't think they had too much contact with the record company before.' In fact Mobbs believes that Floyd, in the days before websites, downloads and YouTube, were signed to a record company for only one reason. 'They had to have a record company otherwise their records wouldn't come out but there was never much contact.'

And as the band moved into making the new album, the man who would go on to sign the Sex Pistols to EMI – where they famously declared that they wouldn't go on to the Harvest label as it was 'full of hippy shit' – knew there was a limit to his involvement. 'I never considered that I or anyone at EMI would have any A&R involvement over Floyd. By this time they were in command of the whole thing.'

But, in fact, the band was not in command of everything. Their manager was Steve O'Rourke who, in 1968, had taken over the reins from Pete Jenner and Andrew King, the pair who had first put the band under contract via Blackhill Enterprises in 1966. O'Rourke's arrival had followed in the wake of founding member Syd Barrett's departure and the arrival of Dave Gilmour.

Jenner, a graduate of Cambridge University who went on to manage Roy Harper, Ian Dury, The Clash and Billy Bragg, takes the view that anonymity was one of the major reasons for Floyd's success in the wake of Barrett being fired. 'Being anonymous helped them get over the fact that Syd left. He was absolutely the frontman and that was why I chose to look after Syd', he says. Tragically not even Jenner could keep Barrett away from the damaging influence of drugs. 'He was gorgeous, the lead singer and he wrote all the songs but sadly he was far more seriously damaged than anyone knew.'

O'Rourke, who trained as an accountant and emerged as Pink Floyd's booking agent, had a role that was easily identified by Mobbs and his colleagues at Harvest and EMI. 'Steve was the band's hustler, their wheeler dealer businessman who would get the deals done without ever getting involved in anything creative', explains Mobbs before adding, 'And I got on pretty well with him.'

The band's fourth US tour – a 17-date affair opening at the Fort Hesterly Armory in Tampa, Florida – included two concerts at New York's prestigious Carnegie Hall on the first two days of May and in the audience was Billboard correspondent – and future editor — Sam Sutherland. Picking up on the band's five-year haul to get to this stage, he wrote '… those years of steady work particularly on the UK college circuit have forged a group of exemplary stability and undeniably effective showmanship.'

He went on to say, 'Determining just when Pink Floyd's musical expertise leaves off and their electronic powers begin is really beside the point for the band's use of elaborate electronic effects is perfectly suited to their sinister atmospheric use of harmony and texture.' Explaining that the band included a new piece called 'Eclipse' in the set, Sutherland concluded that the show was 'very powerful, evoking War of The Worlds, but beautifully timed and presented with no little humor.'

DARK SIDE OF THE MOON REVEALED

Chapter Four

After their two-and-a-half week trip to the States, it was time for Floyd to return to Abbey Road for a month-long session of recording, starting on May 24 1972. A minor downpage news story in the June 3 issue of Melody Maker reported on their progress and stated that the working title of the new Pink Floyd album had changed from '*Dark Side of the Moon*' to '*Eclipse*' and the item also announced – optimistically – that the scheduled release date for the album would be in August.

The issue of whether to be 'Dark Side' or not to be 'Dark Side' came about thanks to the folk-rock band Medicine Head and their 1972 album release. Leader John Fiddler had formed the band with Peter Hope-Evans in 1968 and had already chosen the title *Dark Side of the Moon* for their release. 'It was the devastating feeling of loss that I had', explains Fiddler whose lyrics for the title song included the line 'I feel like I'm living on the *Dark Side of the Moon*.'

When Medicine Head's album hit the shops, Floyd opted to use 'Eclipse' – the song that Waters had declared should be the album's ending – as their new working title. When Medicine Head's album failed to make any noticeable impression in the charts, Floyd took the opportunity to drop the name '*Eclipse*' and use the original title once again. 'It didn't sell well so we thought what the hell', said Gilmour at the time, while Fiddler confirms that he was never contacted about the title.

'We have never had a conversation about the title,' he confirms before adding that to this day he still bears no grudges. 'I have never been annoyed about their use of the title, it just verifies the fact that is a very strong title.'

Interestingly Nick Mobbs, the head of the band's label, seems to think that it was the band's bass player who told him of the final decision over the album's title. In his address book from the time he has written, on the page for entries under W, the words 'Dark Side of the Moon' above the entry for 'Roger Waters'. 'It suggests to me that Roger was the first person to tell me that was what the album was going to be called. That's the only reason I can think of as to why I wrote it on the W page.'

With the album now officially *Dark Side of the Moon* titled *Dark Side of the Moon* both the word 'Eclipse' and the compelling tag line 'A Piece For Assorted Lunatics' were finally edited out of the picture – Pink Floyd's return to Abbey Road was welcomed by the then-deputy studio manager Ken Townsend. He had, like many of EMI's staff, got to know Floyd through not just their recordings and releases but also the cricket matches held each year which pitched the record company against the rock band.

With the studio now boasting 16-track machines, Townsend recalls his role in Floyd's return. 'I was no doubt involved in organising how they were going to make the album with two 16-track machines', he says before explaining how the machines were utilised. 'We transferred some tracks on to a second 16-track machine and left some tracks spare and then we bounced between them all. It was quite complex but I was keen on our engineers doing things to get the best results for the artists using the studio.'

Townsend, who ultimately went on to serve as studio manager, also acknowledged the work carried out by EMI's biggest ever band The Beatles some years earlier. 'What Floyd did was carry on from what The Beatles had done five years earlier when they used two 4-track machines but in a bigger way. They were quite complex technical sessions.' Townsend's connection with The Beatles went all the way back to June 1962, and the group's first commercial test for EMI.

Another Abbey Road and EMI employee who was destined to end up working on *Dark Side of the Moon* was engineer Alan Parsons, and Townsend recalls that he had a role in Parsons' appointment as well. 'Alan had tape-oped for Floyd on *Atom Heart Mother* in 1970 and was showing a bit of talent so he was now right for sessions,' he adds. The process also involved Vera Samwell, the person responsible for overseeing studio bookings and assigning engineers to each session at Abbey Road between 1941 until her retirement in 1979.

'It seemed like an obvious choice for me to work on the album because I had worked with them before' recalls Parsons, 'but it would have been Vera who ultimately told people that they would do this session with that act.'

Although he had not seen the band's stage shows at the Rainbow, once he was on the radar to work on the album Parsons made a point of seeing the band's live rendition of their new work before he began working on tracks such as 'Us and Them', 'Money', 'The Great Gig in the Sky' and 'Time' at Abbey Road during the summer of 1972. 'I had no specific brief as to what I should as engineer and I wasn't very good at keeping my mouth shut' he says. 'The traditional role of an engineer is to do what's he's told to do by the producer and not offer an creative input other than on sound issues.'

'It's every engineer's nightmare having four guys to work with as producers but the five of us made a good team', continues the man who went on to create the multi-million selling Alan Parsons Project. And if working with four band members who were also acting as producers was complicated so, it seems, were the sessions. 'It was complex', recalls Parsons. 'With second generation 16-track, a lot of the so-called cross fades were allowed for on the multi-track and it was recorded as a continuous piece on the multi-track, song by song. It went to a second generation 16-track in order to mix the first 16-track down to make more tracks available.'

The work, which saw cables running along corridors into machines outside the Studio 3 control room or even into machines in other studios, was, in Parsons' words, 'fairly high demand stuff which definitely tested Abbey Road to the limit.' And, according to studio manager Ken Townsend it was all very reminiscent of life at the studio a decade earlier. '*Dark Side of the Moon* did stretch Abbey Road to the limits just as The Beatles had earlier.'

With its control room perched up a flight of stairs away from the well of the studio, giant movable baffle boards and linen bags full of seaweed hanging from the walls to help the acoustics, Abbey Road Studio 2 was the place where The Beatles had recorded so many of their hit singles and albums and was probably, by the end of the sixties, the world's most famous studio.

But Pink Floyd refused to be overawed by their famous surroundings. 'The myth about The Beatles and Studio 2 didn't affect me' was what Gilmour once told this author. 'It was just a studio. It never really occurred to me that The Beatles had used it … although they certainly put Abbey Road on the map.' Inspired or not, Floyd still opted for Studio 2 as the location for most of the recording of Dark Side as engineer Parsons recalls:

'We did most of it in Studio 2 with some recording and mixing in Studio 3', he says before explaining how Studio 1 – the giant studio used mainly for classical recording – was utilised. 'The piano on

'The Great Gig in the Sky' was a Steinway concert grand which was in Studio 1 but we used Studio 2's control room. This caused some hilarity when Rick thought he was playing with the rest of the band in number 2 but it was actually a tape playback. In the middle of the take we all went up to behind him and shouted 'boo!''

Among the first tracks recorded during the sessions which ran from May into June was 'Us and Them', a combination of Wright's instrumental track and Waters' lyrics with Gilmour's lead vocals over backing vocalists Doris Troy, Lesley Duncan, Liza Strike and Barry St John alongside the saxophone of Dick Parry.

It's interesting to note that four years after Syd Barrett's idea of adding two saxophones and a girl singer to the band's line-up had been dismissed by Waters as another madcap scheme from their guitarist's troubled mind, Floyd now brought in one saxophone and four girl singers to help expand the sound.

All four singers had plenty of experience: New Yorker Troy had worked with The Drifters, Solomon Burke and The Rolling Stones; Strike had credits on albums by Stephen Stills, Bryan Ferry and Elton John; St John (real name Elizabeth Thompson) had recorded with Rod Stewart, Elton and Mott The Hoople, while Duncan was a songwriter and singer for Dusty Springfield. But not all of them found working on *Dark Side of the Moon* an overwhelmingly enjoyable experience.

'It was very serious. This was very quiet,' recounts Strike. 'There was no interchange between people.' Duncan also put her feelings on the record about sharing the studio with Pink Floyd. 'They weren't very friendly. They were cold, rather clinical', she explained. 'There were no smiles, we were all quite relieved to get out.'

For saxophonist Dick Parry the new gig with Floyd came as a result of his long-time friendship with Gilmour — who he played with in the local Cambridge group Jokers Wild in the mid-sixties

- before embarking on a career as a successful session musician. After Dark Side he went on to feature on two more Floyd albums in addition to a host of live tours.

Although the finished tracks would finish up on *Dark Side of the Moon*, there were songs which, at this stage, had alternative working titles. 'Breathe In The Air' was called 'Travel' while 'The Great Gig in the Sky' was known as 'Religion'. ''Brain Damage', meanwhile – a song in memory of Barrett and earlier days in Cambridge - was originally called 'The *Dark Side of the Moon*' before becoming known for a time as 'The Lunatic Song'. Waters' early song 'Money', reportedly first demoed with the sound of loose change revolving on his wife's potter's wheel, now featured bags of cash being dropped on the studio floor and the ringing sound of a cash register.

Meantime, the combined sound of clocks chiming and ticking was a highlight on 'Time'. Engineer Parsons had recorded the timepieces as part of a demonstration for the new quadraphonic sound system. 'I recorded them in a watchmaker's shop with a portable tape machine and did each one separately, ticking and then chiming,' he recalls. In fact, according to Townsend, Abbey Road had a long history of recording sound effects for possible use by clients. 'Every time we went anywhere with a mobile we used to take a little portable tape recorder and record things. We had seagulls from Blackpool and I used to record steam trains on Taplow railway station.'

During the making of *Dark Side of the Moon*, Floyd regularly raided Abbey Road's famous collection of sound effects. 'They just played around with lots of things we had in there', says Townsend. But it wasn't just sound effects that Floyd experimented with for their new album. Waters had the idea of introducing spoken word into the songs and he set about drafting questions covering the subjects of madness, violence and mortality. He then set them up on a music stand outside Studio 3 and invited whoever was wandering around the studio to record their answers and observations into a microphone.

Paul and Linda McCartney, Wings guitarist Henry McCulloch, members of Floyd's own crew and studio staff were all featured, although the contribution from the former Beatle was never used as it was considered by the various members of Floyd as 'too clever, too guarded' and also as 'useless' and 'funny, which wasn't what we wanted'.

However, the contributions from Abbey Road's very own Gerry O'Driscoll were among the most memorable. 'Gerry was a star', recalls Townsend. 'He was an amazing bloke who played the accordion in pubs at night and always waffled on about things, he was always saying he wanted to go to the moon.' Employed as porter, cleaner and even night time receptionist, O'Driscoll also had the job of setting up the rostrums and music stands for visiting musicians and he grabbed the opportunity to be part of Waters' vox-pop experiment.

On 'Speak To Me', alongside the manic laughter of Floyd's road manager Pete Watts and the words of roadie Chris Adamson – 'I've been mad for fucking years' – O'Driscoll adds, 'I've always been mad. I know I've been mad like the most of us have' while on 'Eclipse' he adds the immortal lines 'There is no *Dark Side of the Moon* really. As a matter of fact it's all dark.'

But not everyone was happy with the progress Pink Floyd were making on their new album in London's most famous studio. According to long-serving Abbey Road man Ken Townsend there were issues with some fellow members of the creative fraternity. 'They had a few disagreements with people like the classical producer Christopher Bishop who stormed into their studio one night and told them to turn the sound down,' he explains.

Bishop would be appointed Senior Classical Producer at EMI

later the same year and went on to win a Grammy in 1979 as Producer of the Best Classical Record. Townsend remembers that Floyd chose an odd way to respond to his outburst. 'They then put a note on the wall in the studio with every B in 'Bishop' changed to an F. I had to get them all together one day to make the peace as Floyd always claimed that because they sold a lot more records they should be left alone.'

During the summer sessions at Abbey Road, the band's thoughts turned to the subject of album titles and artwork and that meant a call to the team of Powell and Thorgerson at Hipgnosis, Floyd's favourite creative designers. 'We had a working relationship with Floyd since their second album', explains Powell. 'I was very close to Syd in Cambridge and Storm was very close to Roger – so it was the old story of who you know.'

Having worked on all four studio albums from *A Saucerful of Secrets* onwards – *Ummagumma*, *Atom Heart Mother* and *Meddle* - Hipgnosis were summoned to the studio to talk about the new project and it brought back some memories for Powell. 'I had been to their shows at the Rainbow in early 1972 and to be honest I didn't particularly think much of it. It was a new piece and it was a very interesting show but I don't remember the shows turning out exactly as the album.'

And at that first album design meeting in the canteen at Abbey Road, Powell also recalls that the album already had a title. 'From the moment we met with the chaps it was going to be *Dark Side of the Moon*. There was no mention of it being called 'Eclipse',' says Powell, whose company has also produced ground-breaking design work for the likes of Led Zeppelin, Electric Light Orchestra, Bad Company and Wings.

Powell recalls that at that initial meeting the only member of the band who had any idea of what they wanted for the sleeve was Rick Wright. 'He said he wanted something that was more graphic than the work we had done previously', he explains. When the other group members suggested that sounded bit 'chocolate-boxy', Wright apparently told them that he liked things like Black Magic chocolate boxes.

'He wasn't the most creative, graphically speaking' recalls Powell of Wright, 'but it was just that nobody else had any particular ideas. That was how we worked with Floyd – it was often left to us to come up with designs and show them different images.' The upshot, according to Powell, was that everybody eventually went along with the idea that some sort of single graphic image would be 'nice' although he and his partner were far from convinced. 'I remember leaving the meeting with Storm and we were thinking 'What's this, a fucking chocolate box or a Pink Floyd album cover?'

Taking the 'nice' brief on board, Powell and Thorgerson went into full creative mode which often involved working late into the night when nobody else was in their studio. 'We threw ideas around', says Powell, but there was one book that they often turned to for inspiration. 'It was an old photographic book from the 1940s and there was picture in there of a prism, it was a reflection of a prism of sunlight going across a piece of paper. Storm and I saw it together and we both thought 'that looks interesting' and then Storm sketched a triangular shape.'

After that they turned to illustrator and graphic artist George Hardie –'Neither of us could draw for toffee' – and asked him to 'do something with a triangle and a rainbow prism coming out from that.' The resulting prism/pyramid drawing then became one of around half a dozen ideas that Hipgnosis submitted to Floyd for their consideration. 'There was an idea of a Silver Surfer which came straight out of Marvel comics,' says Powell, 'but the prism and the pyramid was an idea which was particularly designed for *Dark Side of the Moon* and nobody else.'.

It took Hipgnosis around a week to get their ideas down on

paper and then it was back to Abbey Road for a second creative meeting with the band. 'This time we met in the actual studio which was all rather moody', Powell remembers. 'We lined the drawings up against an amplifier or along the wall and they all stood there looking at them. Immediately they saw the pyramid/prism image they all went 'that's it', although Rick was actually first and then everybody followed suit.'

The next step was for Hardie to draw the whole thing as an illustration although it still lacked one vital ingredient. 'The band bought into the idea in black and white and shades of grey. They never saw it in colour until it was finished and printed as a sleeve,' says Powell whose partnership with Thorgerson was dissolved in 1983.

Chapter Five

While the Hipgnosis team went away and worked on the design for the sleeve of *Dark Side of the Moon*, Pink Floyd, after taking a lengthy summer break, found themselves on their way to America for a fifth time, but they were unsure of their status with EMI's American company Capitol Records.

Their earlier releases had been assigned to the subsidiary jazz/folk label Tower Records and they were less than happy with Capitol's efforts with their previous releases in the US. *Ummagumma* had peaked at #74 and while *Atom Heart Mother* had climbed to #55, *Meddle* failed to make it past #70 in the States.

All this made the band and manager O'Rourke uneasy about offering the new *Dark Side of the Moon* album to Capitol, which EMI bought as their American arm in 1950. However, while business was being talked about in conference rooms, the band were back making music on stage and the tour which began on September 8 in Austin, Texas took them to a legendary Los Angeles venue.

'The Hollywood Bowl, that was a wonderful show,' was Gilmour's summing up of their band's September 22 performance. Also in the audience that night was British singer, producer and manager Peter Asher who had moved to LA after his spell as head of A&R for The Beatles' Apple label. 'I remember seeing them do the show at the Hollywood Bowl and thinking how cool it was that we never actually get to see them. You barely saw them and that mystique was undoubtedly a big part of their success.'

Another Englishman who was in the audience that night was long-time EMI Music Publishing executive Terry Slater. He was living in California by 1972 and running Capitol's music publishing arm Beechwood Music, and recalls not just the show but also how strained the relationship was between the band and their record label:

'When they played Hollywood Bowl they disliked Capitol so much that they didn't want anyone from the label there. They only allowed me and Rupert Perry [Capitol's resident English executive] to have tickets and we took along Peter Asher,' says Slater. 'And Floyd were happy to see us there.' While Perry doesn't recall an actual ban on the US label's execs going to the gig, he does look back on it as an uncomfortable period in the relationship between the band and their record company. 'We had to deal with the overriding issue that Pink Floyd did not like Capitol and did not want to be on Capitol,' he says.

'It all dated back to when their first two albums came out and Capitol stuck them on a small label called Tower. That really upset them and going backstage even to say hello was not a good experience. I was always petrified of going back to see them, and having a relationship with a record company was something that never bothered them.'

While he has no recollection of the band's animosity towards Capitol, Asher did sense that at least one band member might have made his feelings known. 'I would say that Roger isn't the kid of person who is frequently happy with his record company.'

Formerly half of Peter & Gordon, whose 'A World Without Love' hit number one in both the UK and the US in 1964, Peter Asher had been a follower of Pink Floyd since their days at London's UFO club and he recalls a later get-together in Los Angeles. 'I used to see them in passing in the States when we were doing different things but I do remember sitting and having a drink with them at Le Dome restaurant in LA, and it might even have been after the Hollywood Bowl show.

'I was with Nick and Roger,' recounts Asher, 'and I suddenly realised that 90% of the people in the room didn't know they were in the band. They had total facial anonymity ... I was sitting with Pink Floyd and nobody else cared or knew – and they loved it.'

Gilmour's recollections of the band's US tour in the autumn of 1972 made reference to their stage presentation and the fact that back then it was just the four of them on stage. 'We still didn't have any films to go with *Dark Side of the Moon*,' he says while also pointing out that they didn't always play to sold out houses in America. To make things look more impressive they hired, for their Los Angeles shows, a battery of the searchlights used at Hollywood film premiers which they then fanned out backstage and pointed skywards. 'It looked fantastic,' remarked Gilmour.

Using films to go with the music during live concerts was not a new idea in 1972 and it was something that Floyd were keen to pursue as they worked on Dark Side but it was down to a student at the Birmingham College of Art to come up with the first visual interpretation of Floyd's music.

Ian Emes had begun making Super 8mm films featuring psychedelic lighting effects and 'strange semi-narrative' and setting them to Floyd's music even before he moved into his college's animation department, where he was inspired by The Beatles cartoon film *Yellow Submarine*.

'It was revolutionary back then,' recalls Emes, a BAFTA and Oscar-nominated film maker. But it was during a party in Birmingham that he was further inspired. 'They were playing the new Floyd album and although I wasn't a very druggy person, the room was filled with this dope haze and out of it came *Meddle*.' Inspired and excited by what he heard, Emes immediately started working on a new idea.

'I did a storyboard and made this film called French Windows which was a direct interpretation of the track 'One of These Days',' explains Emes, who went on to make music videos for Duran Duran, Wings, Mike Oldfield and the solo Roger Waters. 'When I saw it, it blew me away. I thought 'What the hell have I made?' and the truth is that I don't think I've made anything better.'

When Emes moved to London soon after making the film, a friend of his submitted his effort to BBC TV's hippest music show *The Old Grey Whistle Test* where series producer Mike Appleton was, by coincidence, busy recruiting visual material from art students in an effort to give 'burgeoning talent access to TV exposure'.

Appleton realised that the chances of Pink Floyd appearing on OGWT to plug their latest release back in 1972 were always going to be slim to say the least, as the band's original manager Pete Jenner confirms. 'I think there was a problem for them with OGWT and coping with all the stuff they put on their records. How to do that live in a TV studio would have been an issue,' he says.

Consequently the show's producer Appleton was happy to receive Emes' film which he thought came direct from the filmmaker although Emes stresses that it was actually submitted by a friend – without his knowledge. 'When it was shown, I watched it but was unaware that thousands of other people might be watching it at the same time.'

The idea of touring the new music from *Dark Side of the Moon* before and during its recording was something else that was not entirely unheard of in 1972, but it did mean that fans had heard and absorbed a live version of the songs before the final version was issued on vinyl. According to Nick Mason, the band's performances in concert were meant to generate a specific feeling. 'There's meant to be a lot of heavy vibes coming off the stage during *Dark Side of the Moon*', said the drummer in 1972, when he also explained the merits of playing the album live before putting it down in the studio. 'I think this is a better way of doing it because you spend more time making a good record.'

By this time both Pink Floyd and their manager knew that they were in the process of making a 'good record' and they were reluctant to deliver it to their American record label. The band's deal with EMI dated back to their original releases on the EMI-owned UK Columbia imprint in 1967 and covered the world but *Dark Side of the Moon* was the last album due under their EMI Records contract which included the licensing of releases to Capitol for North America.

According to Bhaskar Menon, the chairman of Capitol Records at the time, there was a degree of doubt and uncertainty about the band's newest release being delivered to Capitol. 'The doubt and uncertainty arose because Pink Floyd's management had made it known that they had already signed North American rights to the band's future (post Dark Side) albums to CBS,' recounts Menon.

The negotiations revolved around EMI Records retaining the rights to future Floyd albums for territories outside North America and in return allowing *Dark Side of the Moon* to be released in major territories such as the USA, Canada and Japan under their newly negotiated deal with CBS. Rupert Perry, later to join Capitol before becoming chairman of EMI Records UK, was based at EMI's London headquarters in 1971, working for the company's Managing Director L.G. Wood and he was aware of a rift developing between Floyd and EMI.

'In remember that in 1971 Steve O'Rourke came into to meet with L.G. Wood because he really wanted to get out of the deal with Capitol', says Perry. By the time the band began recording *Dark Side of the Moon* in earnest, they were on the verge of signing to CBS whose president Clive Davis had reputedly put an advance of £1 million on the table. CBS, under Davis, was established as one of the most successful record companies in the world with a roster of acts which included Bob Dylan, Janis Joplin, Santana, Simon & Garfunkel and Barbra Streisand.

In an effort to persuade O'Rourke to stay with Capitol, the band were offered an extra 2% over their standard 5% royalty on their next album release *Obscured by Clouds*. And according to Perry the plan almost worked. 'Even though the sales of Obscured weren't huge – they peaked at around 300,000 – Capitol mounted a pretty aggressive campaign and Steve was feeling reasonably OK but he still wanted off the label.'

In the middle of this dispute, Floyd went back into the studios in October 1972 to continue working on *Dark Side of the Moon* although the dual attraction of football and a TV comedy show interrupted the sessions. 'If it was a football night we would always finish early as Roger was into football. He was playing as well as there was a Pink Floyd team', explains Alan Parsons. 'And if Monty Python was on TV we'd have to stop.'

There were also a couple of other people in Abbey Road during the various Floyd sessions. Pete Jenner was busy working in the studio with his new signing Roy Harper (who was making the album *Lifemask* at the same time) and explains, 'I wasn't involved with the album but I bumped into the band in the studio and I became aware of the new material for Dark Side,' while Harvest label manager Mobbs was busy co-producing his first direct signings to the label. 'There was a direct overlap with Floyd being in there and me working with Babe Ruth and I seem to recall hearing a bit of 'Us and Them' which I remember because it was so haunting. In fact every time I popped into see Floyd – and it might have only been for ten minutes at a time – what I heard sounded wonderful.'

DARK SIDE OF THE MOON REVEALED

Chapter Six

With the situation over Pink Floyd in America becoming a major contractual dispute between the band and Capitol Records, the next person to be made aware of the situation was British music publishing executive Terry Slater, a man whose association with Pink Floyd stretched back decades: in addition to playing with the Everly Brothers on a bill with Floyd in Chicago's Kinetic Playground in July 1968, Slater had also been to school with the group's manager, Steve O'Rourke.

'When Steve arrived in Los Angeles in late 1972 he called me up and I invited him over to my house for Sunday lunch,' recalls Slater. And when he arrived, O'Rourke was clutching samples of a new Pink Floyd album. 'Rather than leave them in the Hyatt House hotel – where bands' instruments and albums used to go missing on a regular basis – he brought the tapes with him. When I asked him was the album was like he said 'it's really cool and it's called *Dark Side of the Moon*' and then he added, 'and I'm going to hit Capitol for £300,000'.

O'Rourke explained to Slater that Capitol had 'never gone out on a limb for Floyd' and both he and the band were unhappy with the sales of *Meddle* and *Obscured by Clouds*. 'Steve felt that the company had not done a great job,' says O'Rourke, 'and that nobody in Capitol seemed that keen on Floyd.'

Despite O'Rourke's assertions about the future, Capitol's chairman Menon was hugely committed to the task of establishing Floyd as major stars in North America. 'I had personally, ever since my arrival as chairman in early 1971, brought to bear the highest priority and fully comprehensive and emphatically focused new support strategy on the market for Pink Floyd.' In the light of this support the band, quickly reflected in the improved success of Obscured by Clouds — which became the first Pink Floyd album to enter the US top 50 when it peaked at number 46 – although Menon was perplexed and less than happy to discover what O'Rourke and the artists seemed to have in mind.

'I regarded Pink Floyd's management's position both as an extremely unfriendly and improper use of blackmail in relation to EMI Records (EMIR) who had achieved outstanding success for the band worldwide outside the US right from the start of their professional career,' says Menon, who went onto become chairman of EMI Music Worldwide but who, at this stage, was caught in the middle of EMI Records' dilemma.

'EMIR's management team told me categorically that they could not risk losing contract renewal with Pink Floyd and encouraged me to negotiate direct with the group if I wished to', explains Menon. 'Having little other choice I asked for a meeting with EMIR together with EMI Group's Chief Executive Sir John Read in his office and informed them – seemingly to their relief – that I would take a shot at negotiating direct with the artist and their manager.

'I had got to know both pretty well by then and I made sure it was understood at the meeting in EMI House in London that if I succeeded then *Dark Side of the Moon* would be deemed a directly contracted Capitol Records album and not one obtained by license from EMIR. That would absolve Capitol of paying pressing fees on its sales.'

While he was disappointed in the stance taken by Floyd and O'Rourke, Menon was determined to try and rescue for Capitol Records the upcoming work which he assessed to be 'musically and theatrically a masterpiece which, as an album, would be the overriding classic of Pink Floyd's creative efforts thus far'. With EMI Records refusing to extend their support to Menon's efforts and Capitol Records, in the words of Perry, 'on a bit of a knife edge' with only four US acts (The Band, Grand Funk Railroad, Steve Miller and Helen Reddy) earning US Gold Albums during 1972, Menon drew up his battle plan.

He tracked the band and their manager down to Marseille in southern France where they were in the midst of a series of five performances with Les Ballets de Marseille and director Roland Petit. The show was broken into three parts with 'The Pink Floyd Ballet' as the final section featuring a ballet in four movements, set to the tracks 'One Of These Days', 'Careful With That Axe Eugene', 'Obscured By Clouds', 'When You're In' and 'Echoes'.

By flying from London to Charles de Gaulle Airport in Paris and then internally to Marseille, Menon arrived in the city just as the group went into the final hour of their performance. He and O'Rourke adjourned to what Menon recalls was 'a less than elegant bar which was overcrowded with a large bevy of Algerian and Tunisian ladies and gentlemen engaged in active commerce'.

After a couple of swigs of absinthe, the conversation turned to contracts and agreements with Menon quick to tell O'Rourke that he was certain that EMIR would never give up their rights to Floyd's *Dark Side of the Moon* album in North America – 'though of course I absolutely knew otherwise' – particularly as it would mean adding

79

further to the strength of their global rivals CBS.

At this point, according to Menon, O'Rourke was willing to bet any amount that 'within less than ten minutes of entering EMIR's offices in London he would walk out with a letter from the company giving up their North American rights to the album in question.' Menon's riposte was a one-sided wager in which O'Rourke would receive the head of Capitol's gold wristwatch if he was able to extract such a concession from EMIR and, in addition, if he was prepared to 'commit this one-sided wager to paper – admittedly on a bar napkin'. O'Rourke was also told that even if he didn't manage to get a concession from EMIR over North American rights he would still have no obligations or commitments or payments to make to Menon even though he had lost the bet.

However, the head of Capitol Records also reminded the manager of Pink Floyd that if he did lose the bet then *Dark Side of the Moon* would automatically be delivered to Capitol through the agreement with EMIR. At this point, Menon recalls, there was a genuinely amazed response from O'Rourke who said that he and the band were surprised at Menon's insistence and enthusiasm for wanting Dark Side, even when Capitol knew it would be the last album they would get, as the deal for future albums was already signed and sealed with CBS Records.

With their show over, the band joined the record chief and their manager in the bar and it was then that Menon explained to them all that a plan was already in place. He told them that Capitol had 'already laid the foundation for a total renaissance of Pink Floyd's entire catalogue in North America' and then added that the company 'would fight with all our might to see the conclusion of our efforts with *Dark Side of the Moon* which we believed would be a gigantic success and we wanted to play a direct and leading part in its assured glory.'

Even though he told the band members about the one-sided

wager with their manager, Menon realised that it might take something more substantial to swing things his way. 'I felt quite sure that at that late hour they would need some more tangible and hopefully closing incentive to seal the deal with Capitol.'

It was at this point in the early hours of a new morning in Marseille that Menon put the details of a deal he had worked out on the flight to France. 'I offered two special ad hoc terms – a sizeable additional special advance recoupable only from Capitol's sales of the Dark Side album in North America, and an increased royalty for the album's sales in North America.'

Menon put this offer on the table feeling entirely confident that the additional special advance (rumoured to be as much as £500,000), though substantial was, in his view, as a creative business judgement 'almost completely risk-free'. There was also a higher royalty rate (which some estimates put at around 13%), the same gross rate (artiste royalty plus inter-company pressing fee) which Capitol would have been obliged to pay EMIR if the Dark Side album was secured by license for North America, rather than directly as now proposed..

As Menon proceeded to produce two new napkins and scribbled down the basic terms on offer, he reminded O'Rourke that if he didn't accept this direct special offer then Capitol would get the album anyway through EMIR, and there would be no additional special advance and no higher royalty rate for North America sales. Earlier he had also emphasised the importance of Capitol's new marketing strengths and strategies which the group had witnessed and stressed the potential destabilisation that inevitably came with changing labels – which, he added 'should not even be contemplated with such a monumental work as *Dark Side of the Moon.*'

After the band and manager had conferred in the corner of the bar, Menon recounts what happened at shortly after 4am, in the final hours before the bar shut. 'They came to my table to confirm their acceptance of the special terms and Capitol's special North American deal on offer for the *Dark Side of the Moon* album. We shook hands, hugged and signed and exchanged each other's bar napkins on which the special terms had been briefly memorialised before making our fatigued, and my exuberant, way to our beds.'

Although he awoke the next morning with a major hangover, Menon recalls that also had 'the overwhelming satisfaction of knowing that one of the greatest iconic albums of the rock 'n' roll era had been secured for Capitol for North America.' He also knew deep down that what he had done brought with it 'minimal if any risk' to both EMI and Capitol. 'I can't imagine that the EMI executives knew what the terms of the deal were or what the financial consequences were. Everybody, including myself, was simply relieved.'

§

The earlier lack of film material which concerned David Gilmour, and the broadcast on TV of Ian Emes' personal interpretation of Floyd's music, eventually resulted in a meeting between the rock band and the young filmmaker. 'Sometime after it was shown I got a call', recalls Emes. 'I think Rick Wright had seen it on *The Old Grey Whistle Test* and told the others about it, and then Steve O'Rourke got in touch saying the band wanted to see the film.'

Bizarrely it seems that it was left to Emes to hire a preview theatre (he chose Bijou in Soho's Wardour Steet) and set up the showing. 'Floyd came in very quietly and very politely said hello and sat down to watch the film. I was feeling very nervous', add Emes who then had to experience the band's guitarist sitting next to him throughout the showing of his visual interpretation of their five minute-plus track 'One of These Days'.

'Dave Gilmour came and sat next to me,' says Emes, 'drumming his fingers to the track on his seat. When it was finished he leant over and said 'Did you cut something out?' I told him that I had to as I could only make a four-minute film.' Emes then wondered if it had all gone badly wrong. 'I thought they were upset with me about that but they weren't and they all said 'thank you' and just filed out of the theatre.'

Soon after, manager O'Rourke was on the phone again. 'He asked me to go and talk to them about doing some films for *Dark Side of the Moon*,' says Emes, 'and what they liked in particular were the clocks I used in French Windows.'

While the making of the music progressed in the studio and the plan to create some new films was set in motion, Powell and his Hipgnosis team were busy working on the artwork for the new cover to *Dark Side of the Moon* and they now had a new idea. 'We wanted to put posters and stickers inside as an extra giveaway and the band were really up for that', recalls Powell who further explains the attraction. 'Because they didn't flaunt their image, people didn't know what they looked like so to give some sort of strange stickers and posters away was all part of the imagery.' And as the now accepted Dark Side symbol looked like a pyramid, the design team had a new idea.

'I remember Storm suggesting to Roger,' Powell continues, 'that we go and shoot some infrared film of pyramids in Egypt and him saying 'Great idea, off you go'. So off we went to Egypt with our respective girlfriends for a week in Cairo.' They all booked into the five-star Shepheard Hotel – 'EMI probably paid for it', he suggests – and took pictures of the pyramids during both the day and night. 'We had a ball and it was an Hipgnosis policy in those days to go places and have pictures on album covers that were unusual', he says before explaining that the next step was to get their favourite artist George Hardie to 'draw up some stickers with pyramids and palm trees.'

Harvest label boss Nick Mobbs was a man who quickly recognised the importance of Hipgnosis in the Pink Floyd story 'They were the main creative people,' he says and as work on the album cover progressed so did the potential for problems within EMI. Back in 1972, Floyd had pushed EMI to the limit with their ideas for *Meddle* which included a demand to feature no information on the sleeve. 'My memory is that they wanted the cover to have no writing on it all – not even a record number', explains Mobbs. 'I told them that it wouldn't work in a record shop when people were actually trying to buy their records. I think it was me who persuaded them to have a title, their name and a number on the spine.'

While Mobbs' commercial protestations didn't actually clash with Hipgnosis' creative ideals, the designers were more sympathetic to their clients' wishes than to the demands of the record company. 'We were very precious and as far as we were concerned we never wanted to see on any album cover either a picture of the band or the band's name,' explains Powell. 'We believed – probably arrogantly – that our images stood up on their own and this was always a big debate with record companies and although we weren't deliberately anti-record company we did have a difficult relationship with the companies and EMI was no exception.'

Apart from them wanting album artwork done by the in-house art departments which most of the major record companies retained during the sixties and seventies, the labels also, according to Powell, had their own opinion as to what a record cover should look like. 'Their idea was to have a photograph of the group on the front with the name and title plastered as big as possible. We were totally anti-establishment in that respect and never wanted to see that as we believed that the images were strong enough to stand upon their own and would be seen in a record shop and be instantly identified with the group. And it definitely worked with Floyd and

Led Zeppelin.'

Gered Mankowitz is a photographer who has worked with best selling acts such as The Rolling Stones, Jimi Hendrix, Eric Clapton, Elton John, Cliff Richard, Kate Bush and Wings, and he has a different view as to what expect from an album cover. 'I wanted to change the look of bands from the smiling glossy glittery look to one that was gritty, individual, threatening, sexy and moody. I thought our role was as image makers to the music industry if you like, but Hipgnosis had a terribly pragmatic artistic approach and in my opinion they didn't really give a shit about the music or the subject.'

For Mankowitz, who first toured America photographing The Stones in 1965, album artwork was all about one thing. 'Everybody knew that the purpose of the exercise was to sell records. It was a commercial business for me and other designers and photographers but maybe it was less so for Hipgnosis.'

And while he admits to never knowing or working with the Hipgnosis team, Mankowitz also retains a strong opinion about their work and reputation. 'My overall feeling was that they were incredibly arty and they got away with murder – and I could never understand how they got the budgets to do what they did.' That said, he is quick to praise the imagery that he eventually saw on Floyd's *Dark Side of the Moon* album. 'I think it did work and I think it was probably perfect for them and the album. Whether the ideas were created for the album or came out of the file, it worked and was very well executed.'

As the album artwork was taking shape, Mobbs was contacted by Thorgerson and persuaded to take part in a bizarre contest. 'Storm said to me that the whole thing was going to be a big departure for Floyd and there was going to be a competition for the new artwork.' The designer apparently explained that about a dozen sleeve designers were asked to tender their ideas for artwork for *Dark Side of the Moon* on the basis that they only got paid if their work was chosen.

'Storm then called me over,' says Nick Mobbs, 'and asked me to judge the designs. I went straight to the artwork with the pyramid and prism and said 'Definitely that one', and then Storm just said, 'That's good Nicky, that's good because it's ours and it was always going to be the cover anyway'. To this day I don't know whether they or the band had already chosen it — or even if there ever was a competition.'

1972 drew to close with Pink Floyd's plans for the cinematic premiere of their Pink Floyd Live at Pompeii film being disrupted. Its debut showing at the Rainbow Theatre in London was cancelled at short notice when theatre owners the Rank Organisation discovered that the film had not been granted a certification by the British Board of Film Censors. Three thousand ticket holders were denied the chance to see a film which had already been shown at the Edinburgh Film Festival in September. Undaunted the band set off on a short tour of Europe with dates in France, Belgium and Switzerland before preparing for the final burst of recording their album.

Chapter Seven

When Pink Floyd returned to Abbey Road on January 9 1973, there was a newcomer in the ranks. Chris Thomas had begun his career in 1967 working for George Martin at AIR Studios in London's Oxford Circus on records including The Beatles' '*White Album*', but by 1972 he had taken to operating as a freelance producer..

Having seen Floyd perform at London's Rainbow Theatre in February 1972, Thomas was approached by the band's manager, Steve O'Rourke. 'He called me up and mentioned this story about the band going into the studio with a number of different people in order to choose what kind of mix they wanted. He was alluding to something like that for me.' And when it came to a contract and recompense for his time in the studio, Thomas learnt that O'Rourke had a plan in mind. 'He was talking to me about compensating me if they didn't use my work – it was going to be £1,000 – but I said that I didn't want anything if they didn't use my work,' says Thomas, who was less than happy about the idea of an in-studio competition between producers.

'It seemed a totally ludicrous idea,' he continues, 'and I thought that the band must have known what they wanted and weren't just going to palm it out to anybody.' He had come on board as 'another voice to be there for mixing' but, as he was not an engineer, Thomas took the view that his work would be as a producer and concluded that 'the mention of the other people was a bit of a ruse'.

When the band were in the studio briefly in October 1972, they ran off a tape of what they had recorded to date and sent that over to Thomas in advance of him officially coming on board in early 1973. Looking back the producer was surprised by what he heard on that early tape. 'I was a fan of the Floyd from them doing something like 'Echoes' and was really fascinated by them doing long pieces of instrumental music, and I thought I was going to be working on a Floyd album that was going to be something like that,' he explains.

But when he heard their efforts on the material intended for *Dark Side of the Moon*, Thomas was somewhat taken aback. 'I was surprised to find out that it was going to be songs – they didn't write songs as such, they wrote pieces of music. The stuff they sent to me was all songs and when I said this later in a magazine interview I got hate mail saying 'What do you mean it was just a bunch of songs, it's the greatest album that's ever been made'.'

Surprised or not, Thomas joined Gilmour, Mason, Waters, Wright and engineer Alan Parsons in Abbey Road in the first month of 1973 in order to complete the recording of the album. And while he realised that his arrival meant there would be some friction in the studio, he categorically denies some of the stories that went hand in hand with his attendance. 'The rumours about band members not being in the studio are a load of rubbish – they were all there – and the rumour about me being there to sort out a dispute going on between David and Roger is also absolutely untrue. There was no dispute, there were no different versions, it was a general cooperative thing.'

Without being given any specific brief by the band – 'It was basically a case of do what you fancy, whatever you like' – Thomas was sensitive about the role being played by Parsons. 'Alan felt his toes had been trodden on by my arrival – he was definitely put out. One of the things that I did - and I fought Alan over it because he hated it – was compressing stuff. I loved the sound of compression because it made it sound powerful and Alan hated that – there was a bit of fight over that.'

While he doesn't refer to the issue of compression, Parsons remains unconvinced about Thomas's contribution to Dark Side. 'They thought they needed a fresh pair of ears. They thought we were all too close to it but I don't think it was a good move', says the man who went on to produce back-to- back UK number one hits for Pilot ('January') and Steve Harley ('Come Up And See Me (Make Me Smile)') in 1975. 'I think the album would have been just as good without him. He didn't do very much that was new, we just sat and mixed just like we would have done without him.'

While band members Mason and Gilmour would both later applaud the engineering and production talents of Parsons, Gilmour did also go on record to admit, 'But we would have got there with any good engineer operating the knobs and buttons.'

And on the occasion of the album's 25th anniversary, Parsons who now lives in California and regularly tours with his Project line-up, took the opportunity to give his assessment of the part played by each of the band members in its making.

He deemed Gilmour to be 'the most musical' and the man who dealt with 'musical parts, timing and whatever' while Mason he saw as 'the guiding light in matters to do with the overall atmosphere' and someone who was 'very good on sound effects and psychedelia and mind-expanding experiences.' And while he judged Wright to be 'a little less creatively involved on the production, he took more of a back seat', he explained that Waters was 'concerned with performances, ambiences' before adding, 'He and David produced each other. It was difficult to say who was the leader.'

At the same time, as he judged Parsons to be 'a jolly good engineer', Waters summed up what he saw as the engineer's contribution in the following words. 'I'm sure he had a certain input. But the effect Alan had on *Dark Side of the Moon* is less relevant than the effect *Dark Side of the Moon* had on Alan.'

While the band and their helpers were busying themselves in the studio, Powell and his creative colleagues at Hipgnosis were putting the finishing touches to the artwork for the new album and the idea of having no identification anywhere on the album had finally taken a firm hold with both designers and musicians alike. 'We worked for very powerful bands at the time', says Powell. 'And at that time Pink Floyd were powerful enough to say to their record company, 'If Hipgnosis don't want our name on the cover then nor do we.' They were incredibly supportive of us.'

Acknowledging that in Nick Mobbs both Hipgnosis and Floyd had an in-house supporter at EMI, Powell recalls that their idea was for Dark Side to be delivered to the record buyer in the style of a present. 'The concept was not to show the album cover and create something that when you bought it, a bit like a Christmas present, you had to tear the wrapping off to get at it.' In order to achieve this, the album had to be covered and Mobbs thinks he may have come up with a solution.

'The band pushed everything a bit further with Dark Side and said that they really would like to do it with nothing at all on the sleeve – not on the back, the front or down the spine. So I think I may have come up with the idea of shrink wrapping it in plastic and putting a sticker on the outside.' Mobbs recalls how the band reacted to the idea. 'They accepted it reluctantly and only after the argument, 'You do want to sell records don't you?''

The importance of record covers to music fans in the days before Compact Disc-size reproductions was well understood by Powell as he reflects on the merits of shrink wrapping the album. 'Records and record covers were incredibly precious to people in those days and we knew that some people would respectfully slice the side of the plastic just to get the record out while others might just tear the wrapping off. But if it had a label on it, the people would probably preserve it and to this day I still see album jackets which have still got the plastic cover and the sticker on them.'

The delivery to EMI of the final artwork for *Dark Side of the Moon* involved conversations with Ron Dunton, the company's creative services manager, and that sparked issues for Powell and his team. 'He was old school and his claim to fame was that he worked on all The Beatles' album covers. Then us young hippies came in and said 'Fuck off, roll over old man, you're not in the same league as us.' There was a certain arrogance on our part but we did have the power of the bands behind us.'

Paul Watts, who was in EMI's marketing department at the time, also recalls that the artwork for Dark Side was the subject of a major confrontation. 'The hardest bit was negotiating the situation between Storm from Hipgnosis and Ron Dunton over the artwork and Ron always made a point of being as difficult as possible with Storm.' Dunton's negative attitude towards the designer stemmed from the fact that Storm apparently delivered artwork in, what Watts described as, 'odd bits and pieces that had to be assembled.'

With Storm giving as good as he got and being 'equally spiky', Watts was then left to oversee matters. 'I inevitably had to try and referee the discussion, especially if it was in the afternoon and Ron had been round to the Cricketer's Club for lunch!'

In addition to a cover with no words and no pictures, there was also the issue of what to put in the centre of the double gatefold sleeve. Hipgnosis had the idea to run the rainbow used on the front cover across the centre in what Powell describes as 'a sort of heartbeat pulse'. When they presented their idea to the band 'with lines going straight or converging into a complex shape or something', Waters came up with an idea. 'Roger said he loved the idea of a pulse to go with this and said 'Why don't you try it like a cardiograph?' which we did. I think it looks great but I'm not sure Storm ever liked it.'

The final part of the artwork jigsaw came with the printing of a blue triangle on the centre label of the record and that was once again an Hipgnosis idea. 'Labels were important in those days', recalls Powell who considered it his company's job to deliver the 'complete *Dark Side of the Moon* package.' However, it seems that nobody can remember exactly how many albums were pressed with the blue triangle. 'I have no idea why we did it and I have no idea how many we printed with the triangle on the label' admits Nick Mobbs before adding, 'Maybe Hipgnosis just said they'd do a few with a blue triangle on it but for no particular reason. They were on the band's side and I was happy with that – and Floyd were in charge of every thing.'

While Powell remains 'happy that the package came out in its entirety', he too is unsure about numbers. 'The number of albums that had that blue triangle image on the label was all down to money. If we could get away with the first 50,000 or even 100,000 that was fine but I have to say that record companies were not always totally straight with us and would say things were in or on a certain number of pressings, and then six months later some bits would be missing but we were just happy that it came out in its entirety.'

(*A look at the price guide in Record Collector shows an original 1973 pressing of Dark Side of the Moon with the limited-edition blue triangle label – plus the posters and stickers – at a price of £500 and*

*those in the business of trading in vinyl reckon that could mean that
no more than 10,000 were pressed.)*

§

During his stint in the studio in January and February 1973, Chris
Thomas worked on the tracks 'Brain Damage', 'Eclipse', 'On the
Run', 'Any Colour You Like', plus 'Money' and 'The Great Gig in the
Sky'. For the latter, an instrumental piece by Wright, session singer
Clare Torry was brought in by Alan Parsons to contribute a unique
vocal contribution. Recalling her time in the studio, Torry went on
record to say that her work seemed to make little or no impression
on the band. 'Other than Dave Gilmour I got the impression they
were infinitely bored with the whole thing. When I left I remember
thinking that it would never see the light of day.'

Not only did she make it on to the album but Torry also recorded
in her diary the details of her work on Sunday January 21 1973:
'EMI, 7-10, £30 + credit on Pink Floyd LP.' While her fee was double
the usual amount because it was a Sunday session, the whole
thing left her with a less than satisfactory feeling and in 2012 she
summed up her work on the record with the words: 'In the great
scheme of things my contribution was but a small cog in a much
bigger wheel. Technically it's very good … thank you Alan Parsons.
An enjoyable and important moment? No!'

Over thirty years after she recorded her piece for the album,
Torry, who sang the theme tune to the 1970s TV series *Butterflies*
and also sang with Dolly Parton, Culture Club and Meat Loaf,
took Pink Floyd and EMI to court. She claimed she was owed
songwriting royalties on the basis that the vocal contribution she
made to 'The Great Gig in the Sky' had been 'composed' by her. In
2005 an out of court – and undisclosed – settlement was reached in
her favour and since that time all copies of the album have carried
a writer's credit of Wright/Torry.

While Thomas recalls Torry coming in for 'The Great Gig in the

Sky' segment he hadn't been fully briefed on what to expect. 'I wasn't told that was going to happen so it was a bit odd and as she didn't know them it must have been very difficult for her to go in there and wail. I couldn't quite work out was going on.' He does, however, recall his work on the classic track 'Money' when he was determined to make the guitars 'sound massive'.

Recalling it as 'one definite change I made in terms of producing', Thomas explains, 'There was no double tracking on 'Money' and I said that we had to double-track a riff so there's one on each side of the stereo to build it up and make it really big.' But he further reflects that 'Mr Gilmour might deny that and say it was his idea.'

In addition to working with Pink Floyd in Abbey Road, Thomas was also producing Procol Harum's Grand Hotel album in AIR Studios at the same time, and then he answered a call from Roxy Music. 'We started out on For Your Pleasure with another producer but we really wanted Chris Thomas', says Roxy's Phil Manzanera. The guitarist further recalls being in AIR Studios in January 1973 when he heard Thomas playing back some tracks that weren't Roxy Music songs.

'I knew *Dark Side of the Moon* was going on and then I heard Chris playing 'Money' and I thought it was absolutely fantastic,' says Manzanera, although Thomas isn't exactly sure what Manzanera heard at AIR. 'I have no recollection of taking any tapes away from Abbey Road and doing any work on them in AIR. I must just have been listening back to something for some reason.'

Either way, what he heard in AIR made an impression on Manzanera who, as he recalls, first met a member of Floyd some time around 1968 when he was a 16 year-old schoolboy. 'I really wanted to be a musician and my brother said he knew this guy who had just got into a band and suggested we go and have a chat with him and ask him how you become a professional musician – and that was David Gilmour who had literally just joined Floyd.'

On hearing 'Money' at AIR in 1973, Manzanera was moved to get in touch with the man from Floyd who had influenced his career five years earlier. 'I was brought up on Floyd right from the beginning and knowing somebody from the band – however tenuously – was wonderful for me. I decided to send David a telegram saying, 'Just heard 'Money', guitar solo absolutely amazing. Remember me? I'm in a band now and it's called Roxy Music', and that re-established contact with him.'

DARK SIDE OF THE MOON REVEALED

PINK FLOYD

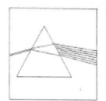

THE DARK SIDE OF THE MOON

A Superb #1 Gold Album SMAS-11163
With A Superb New Single,
"Money" (#3609)

And
A New Tour

June 15 Buffalo, N.Y. (Memorial Aud.)	June 23 Detroit, Mich. (Olympia Stadium)
June 16 Jersey City, N.J. (Roosevelt Stadium)	June 24 Cuyahoga Falls, Ohio (Blossom Music
June 17 Saratoga Springs, N.Y. (Saratoga	Festival)
Performing Arts Center)	June 26 Jonesboro, Geo. (Lake Spivey Park)
June 18 Rain Date for June 16	June 27 Jacksonville, Fla. (Vet. Mem. Col.)
June 19 Pittsburgh, Penn. (Civic Center)	June 28 Miami, Fla. (Pirates World)
June 20, Columbia, Maryland (Merriweather	June 29 Tampa, Fla. (Tampa Stadium)
21 Post Pavilion)	

Right: Pink Floyd with Bhaskar
Menon in the USA for the launch
of *Dark Side of the Moon*

Below: The original blue label
showing *'The' Dark Side of the
Moon*

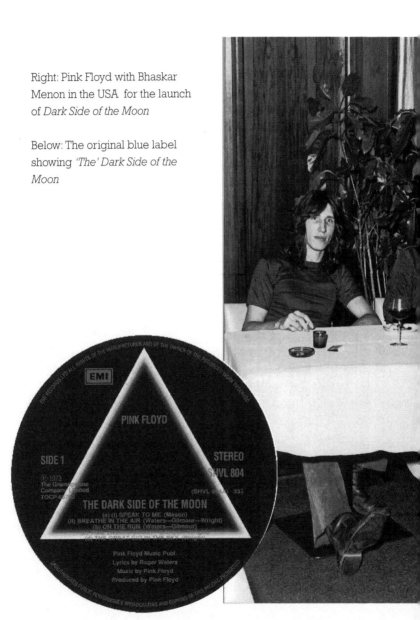

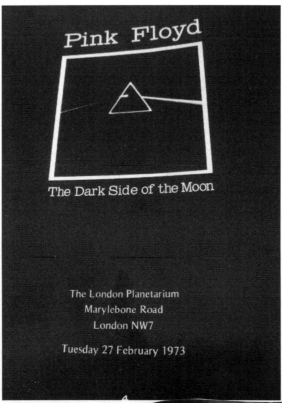

Pink Floyd

The Dark Side of the Moon

The London Planetarium
Marylebone Road
London NW7

Tuesday 27 February 1973

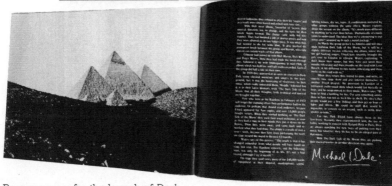

Rare program for the launch of *Dark Side of the Moon* at the London Planetarium in February 1973

Chapter Eight

With *Dark Side of the Moon* nearing completion under the watchful eyes and ears of both Alan Parsons and Chris Thomas, the next item on the agenda was the question of credits on the album sleeve. Even though he was guaranteed his £1,000 fee, Thomas was unhappy with the band's suggestion that it should say 'mixed by Chris Thomas'.

'I thought that was absolutely incorrect,' says Thomas, 'as it was unfair to Alan and implied to some extent that I was engineering the album.' He also realised that the idea of him being credited as co-producer was pretty unlikely. 'The band wouldn't give me any kind of production credit – that was one thing they were vociferous about – so I went to George Martin for his help. I told him it was all a bit weird and asked for his advice. In the end it was George who suggested 'mixing supervised by …' It was a real diplomatic phrase.'

On the other side of the mixing desk, Parsons was being paid by EMI as a staff engineer. 'A pound an hour was what we were paid at the time and I somehow doubt that Chris Thomas got any sort of a royalty', suggests Parsons who correctly assumes, 'He was probably paid a flat fee.'

As the album neared completion so the executives at Capitol Records, who were based in the world- famous Capitol Tower at the junction of Sunset and Vine in Los Angeles, were being geared up for its release. Bhaskar Menon, as he indicated to band manager O'Rourke during their late night 'session' in Marseille, had set up a three-person team to oversee every issue of any consequence whatsoever relating to Pink Floyd. 'I had at least one of them, usually all three of them, report to me direct every single day on all Pink Floyd matters.'

In early February 1973 Menon hosted a lunch in his office in the Tower where executives including Rupert Perry, newly appointed Sales and Promotion Vice President Don Zimmermann, Promotion executive Al Coury and A&R Vice President Maurie Lathower were alerted to the fact that Pink Floyd's manager O'Rourke was coming over from the UK to discuss plans for the new album release.

'It was no secret that the company had failed miserably with earlier albums and Bhaskar told us that he had convinced the band to have Steve meet us and allow us to show him our 'stuff',' recalls Zimmermann. 'And he told us that he negotiated new terms for the album that was arriving. The real drive and focus was firstly to back Bhaskar's commitment and secondly that this new team was as good as anyone and better than most.'

Meanwhile back in London, Chris Thomas, Alan Parsons and Pink Floyd were putting the finishing touches to the album. 'One of the things that was a stroke of genius were the interviews on the album', says Thomas. 'The way it's tied together with all the different links and it was a natural end to the album when he said that about the dark side of the moon … you couldn't top a remark like that, it was the definitive end of the album.' Although he was there at the time the final mixes were done, Thomas had no sense of occasion or impending greatness. 'When you finish something it's just done, you don't go back to it', he says although he does admit, 'You can't see what impact an album might have on other people when you are on the inside of it – it's like Alice Through The Looking Glass but from the other side.'

On the other hand Parsons does recollect that everybody knew something special had happened during the previous year they had spent making the album. 'Whether we all knew we had made an extraordinary album is the most asked question and Roger said in print that he knew it was a mammoth work and I certainly knew that it was their best album to date … but 40 years on the chart, I didn't expect what it has now achieved.'

The importance of Abbey Road Studios, home to number one artists as far ranging as Peter Sellers, Cliff Richard, The Beatles, Kate Bush, The Wurzels and Wings, to the making of *Dark Side of the Moon* is readily and enthusiastically acknowledged by artist manager Pete Jenner. 'The wonderful thing about Abbey Road was that you could get anything if you had a job number – sound effects, extra instruments. It was just the most wonderful place to work and I'm sure it had a lot to do with why Dark Side was so good.' Jenner, who now lectures about the music business to students says simply, 'Nobody else in that period but EMI would have let Floyd sit in the studio for a year making a record which ended with a sleeve with no picture of the band – that was what was so great about EMI.'

Likewise Phil Manzanera, who joined Roxy Music in February 1972 at the same time that Pink Floyd presented their new album at London's Rainbow Theatre, is glowing about the studio's role in the creation of the album. 'The Beatles weren't around doing it anymore so somebody else was taking over the experimentation at Abbey Road and it's incredible that *Dark Side of the Moon* was not made on 24-track.' Explaining that the studios in North London, a cricket's ball throw from the famous Lord's ground, was at the heart of the most innovative recording techniques in the world, he adds, 'It was all a very Heath Robinson British thing but it really worked.'

As the finishing touches were added on the first day of February 1973, so EMI promotions man Martin Nelson re-appeared on the scene to play a vitally important role in the story of the album. 'Nick Mobbs said they were looking for a volunteer to go to Abbey Road and just wait around until Floyd had finished recording the album and then take the tapes to Heathrow Airport.I had specially prepared packaging for it to go as cargo to Capitol Records in LA.'

Arriving at around midnight, Nelson managed to get as far as the studio's reception area but no further. 'The doors into the studios were locked so I sat there with all the packaging stuff until about 2.30am when a tape op came out and asked me what I was doing. He knew that I was coming and took me through into the studio', recalls Nelson who went on to work for both CBS and Universal in a career stretching over 40 years. And once inside the studio he saw Floyd at work putting the finishing touches to their new album.

'They were busy trying to decide how much of the swearing by the Abbey Road doorman/assistant to leave on the album,' recounts Nelson. 'Dave Gilmour was doing most of the editing with razor blades and sticky tape and finally at about 4.30am, they finished, turned the lights down and played it all back. There was just the tape op, the band and me. They listened carefully and nobody said anything and finally I was allowed to drive out to Heathrow at about dawn with the tapes on the car seat and the sound of this incredible music in my ears.'

As the album tapes were being shipped to the States, so the artwork parts were also on their way to Capitol where Creative Services chief Dan Davis was the point of contact for Hipgnosis. 'I was very involved with Po and Storm – although I was closer to Storm – and the salient point was that everything came from them and all usage of that artwork for posters, merchandising or t-shirts had to go to them for approval, and in those days you weren't an act unless you had a t-shirt,' recalls Davis. 'The entire Pink Floyd exercise was run out of the UK and it was all pretty complicated.'

According to Davis the actual sleeve artwork for *Dark Side of the Moon* was never a real problem in America's record shops, where shrink wrapping and stickering were pretty routine, although he does recall some internal objections. 'It was a great sleeve design which I really liked but when it first arrived there were some more staid parts of the company which hated it – 'How can you do something like this, it doesn't say what it is' - but us younger guys loved it.' And Davis also explains that after a while the album was so successful that they didn't need to sticker it anymore 'because everyone knew what it was'.

When Steve O'Rourke arrived in Los Angeles he went along to the offices of Capitol for a meeting in the company's 12th floor conference room when he played the assembled team of executives the album they had paid half a million dollars for. Rupert Perry, who was the only Englishman in the room, readily admits 'I loved the album but I was very biased because I was English and I got on really well with Steve', but insists that everybody else in the room responded in the same way. 'They all just sat there in awe at what they were hearing and it didn't matter how long or short it was, it was a great album.'

Meanwhile Don Zimmermann recalls that the real business started after the playback. 'We were all knocked out by the album and afterwards we met with Steve O'Rourke individually, and in my case I presented him with the marketing and sales plan. To the best of my knowledge they were, in both cases, by far the most ambitious in terms of financial and total commitment that any yet-to-be-broken act had ever received from Capitol.'

While Capitol in America were outlining their plans for the new album, back in the UK EMI were planning a major launch party for *Dark Side of the Moon* – and where better to hold it than at London's famed Planetarium, adjacent to Madame Tussauds famous waxwork museum on Marylebone Road? But as the plans unfolded for the February 27 event, there seemed to be some doubt as to which members of the band were likely to make an appearance.

For Nick Mobbs it was simply a case of 'Maybe someone will come or maybe they won't', and bizarrely it was the band's manager who came up with a solution to a possible no-show by Pink Floyd. 'I think it was Steve who said, as a joke, 'Why don't you just get some cut-outs?' and I liked that idea. We took them from the double spread of the *Meddle* album, so they were already out of date pictures, and made life-size cut-outs which were the first thing that the guests saw as they arrived at the Planetarium.'

Told that the band were definitely not going to show up, it was Martin Nelson who decided to arrange the cut-outs around a table in the reception area and all was well until another piece of news filtered through. 'At some point someone came in and said that the band were coming so we had this mad rush to get rid of the cut-outs before they arrived,' recounts Nelson who adds, 'To this day I don't know if they did all turn up – they could have gone in to the sound booth or into a backroom.'

Mobbs, however, knows for certain that Rick Wright was the only band member who did show up at the lavish launch of their new album and the Harvest executive also denies that there was any dispute over the quality of the sound system used at the launch. 'The story about them not coming because of the quality of the sound system is totally untrue. We brought in a top notch system from Abbey Road to use with the Planetarium light show and to be honest I never thought they would turn up – it was all a bit showbiz for them.'

Writing in his 2005 book *Inside Out*, Nick Mason touched on the

Planetarium event and wrote, 'We were not happy that the record label planned to use a sound system that we didn't consider good enough … we didn't want it played to the press on a sub-standard PA system.' Just for good measure he added, 'The row probably boiled down to a question of money.' However, it seems that what might have been an issue was the fact that a much-vaunted new quadraphonic mix of the album was not finished in time for the launch party and EMI had to use a standard stereo mix thereby possibly alienating the band.

The launch party was announced with a formal invitation announcing:

8-8.40pm – Reception, cocktails in the Arcade

8.45 -9.30pm – The world premiere of the *Dark Side of the Moon* Pink Floyd album beneath the stars of the Planetarium

9.35 – 11pm – Dinner, hot buffet and wine. Drinks and amusements in the Arcade

Melody Maker's Roy Hollingsworth was among the guests and he commented that 'behind a long desk in reception were life-size cardboard cut-outs of Pink Floyd. It was rather surreal – they sat motionless, a normal habit with cardboard', and went on to say, 'What followed presented Floyd as Floyd should be – enormous, massive, overwhelming, impressive.'

Another person invited to the launch party was the band's former manger Pete Jenner and it gave him a chance to finally hear the new album in full – but he came away with some reservations. 'It was a memorable night – I had never been to the Planetarium before – but I did think it was all a bit pretentious. I thought it was shit and that they were so much better when Syd Barrett was writing the songs but that was probably just sour grapes. It crept up on me subsequently.'

In fact as it 'crept up' on him, Jenner came to fully appreciate the Floyd's fifth album without the musician he now managed. 'I don't know whether it was the first concept album but it was certainly a concept album, it has a theme which I thought was all a bit pretentious and really didn't give it a fair crack of the whip at the outset. But through the years, as you kept hearing it, you realised what a fucking great record it is.'

A positive side-effect of EMI's decision to hold a reception in the Planetarium to launch the album was the reaction of some of the guests at the party. Mobbs recalls talking to people during the evening who were 'overawed that we were doing a reception there and were saying 'You must really believe in this album'.'

One man who was not at the Planetarium, despite all his work on the album, was Chris Thomas but he wasn't surprised and simply says, 'Naturally, I wasn't invited to the Planetarium.' Being left off the guest list was one thing but not getting a copy of the album was perhaps an even bigger oversight. 'I was never given a copy of the album when it was finished and I wasn't going to buy one so the first time I heard it was when my next door neighbour bought a copy and I borrowed it from him.'

While he did receive his £1,000 fee for working on the album, Thomas was intent on keeping the money safe. 'I didn't feel like paying for one out of my thousand pounds and the first time I got a copy was when I was in Los Angeles later in the year and I asked Rupert Perry from Capitol for one.'

To this day Thomas sheds no tears over his Dark Side deal and in fact maintains a positive view about his time in the studio with Pink Floyd. 'I have never had any regrets that I just got a grand and no royalty – who else can tell a story like that?' he says before admitting to the one change he did make as a result of working with Floyd. 'I did get Steve O'Rourke to manage me and he did much better deals for me after that.'

When he moved on to work on Roxy Music's For Your Pleasure, Thomas found himself back in charge as producer but his work with Floyd seemingly stayed where it had ended in Abbey Road. 'Chris didn't bring anything from Dark Side to our album,' confirms Phil Manzanera. 'In fact we were most impressed by his work with The Beatles rather than with Floyd where the idea of four musicians as the producers and an engineer must have been an absolute nightmare.'

DARK SIDE OF THE MOON REVEALED

Chapter Nine

Finally, on March 10 1973, *Dark Side of the Moon* was released in America – two weeks ahead of its release in the UK – and it came with some major and imaginative trade advertising in the US music industry's leading magazines.

On page one of Billboard, dated March 3 1973, there was a 5cm square advert showing just the front cover of the album with the line … 'the new album which has been nine months in the making.' Meanwhile the back page carried a full-page colour advertisement featuring a strange amalgam of the album cover plus artwork from the gatefold sleeve together with a list of US tour dates, the Harvest logo and the text: 'Pink Floyd The *Dark Side of the Moon* A superb new work.'

The opening show on the US tour was in fact held at the Dane County Coliseum in Wisconsin's state capital (and second largest city) Madison on March 4 1973. Under the banner headline 'Pink Floyd Clouds Coliseum With Haze Of Space Sound', the local Wisconsin State Journal wrote: 'Once referred to as psychedelic music, Pink Floyd has updated and come around into something loosely labeled space rock, a mixture of some hard driving sets, electronic gimmickry and quadraphonic sound' and they ended up by suggesting, 'No matter how you felt about their music, after watching Pink Floyd's exhausting performance you know 'quiet desperation' doesn't quite make it.'

One man who received an early copy of the new album as soon as it came out in America was Beechwood Music exec Terry Slater and he immediately took the record over to the house of one of closest friends to get his opinion. 'I went out to Phil Everly's house in LA and played it to him all one morning – we just drank black coffee and played the album, says the music publisher. And, according to Slater, the man who, with his brother Don, racked up over a dozen UK and US top ten hits in the fifties and sixties, was mightily impressed. 'Phil freaked out, he got the whole thing and thought it was brilliant.'

While Capitol's creative chief Dan Davis explains that everything to do with Floyd and the new album 'had to be approved by Pink Floyd' - via a route which involved Hipgnosis and EMI in London – Aubrey Powell has a different take on the US trade ad. 'We did all the artwork for the adverts for *Dark Side of the Moon* but the one in Billboard in March 1973 I have never seen and can't imagine that we did it, ' he says before adding, 'It was probably done by Capitol's art department after we submitted an advert which they bastardized – it often happened.'

Although Pink Floyd's previous highest position on the US album charts had been a modest #46, the news about *Dark Side of the Moon* was altogether more encouraging – almost from day one. 'I remember calling Steve O'Rourke and telling him that the album had shipped gold within two days of release,' says Rupert Perry who quickly followed up with some even better news. 'Then I called him again a couple of days later to say it had gone platinum and he was ecstatic because they had never had a US platinum album before.'

As the album, which was officially priced at $5.98, went into shops all across America in early March, Capitol's head of sales Don Zimmermann was anxious to ensure that the dealers had no reason not to stock and promote the new album: 'Dealers everywhere love hits, so with a little incentive – like an extra discount and some advertising money – they stacked them up by the cash register at a good price.'

Soon after, the first reviews began appearing with Billboard proclaiming the new work as 'a tour de force for lyricist Roger Waters' before adding, 'The band is ingrained in a program of heavy introspective statements balanced well by their brooding intensive playing. This is music for intense listening.' Helpfully they finished with a tip for retailers: 'Note to dealers – this is avant-garde rock by one of England's most adventurous bands.'

Meanwhile over at the important and hugely influential Rolling Stone magazine, a young American who would later make a career in Britain as a television presenter and gastronome was giving the album the once-over. 'It seems to deal primarily with the fleetingness and depravity of human life, hardly the commonplace subject matter of rock', said Loyd Grossman. He concluded that '*Dark Side of the Moon* is a fine album with a textural and conceptual richness that not only invites but demands involvement. *Dark Side of the Moon* has flash in the true flash that comes from the excellence of a superb performance.'

Forty years on, Grossman recalls that as a record reviewer for Rolling Stone, Fusion and New York Review of Rock he had 'a particular fascination with more arcane British bands' and he cites King Crimson, Quatermass and Chicken Shack alongside Pink Floyd. While he was aware of 'See Emily Play', Grossman admits that as 'a card carrying member of the counter-culture' he had seen but 'failed to understand' *Zabriskie Point* with its Pink Floyd soundtrack. And as the proud owner of the band's *Atom Heart Mother* album, Massachusetts-born Grossman was also a fan of their artwork. 'As a big Hipgnosis fan, I admired Floyd's taste in album cover design.'

Somebody else who admired the artwork for Dark Side was film maker Ian Emes whose work had captured the attention of Floyd in 1972. 'I love the fact that the artwork has nothing to do with the title,' he says. 'It was a brave thing to do but I don't think they probably thought of it as a brand at the time but it has evolved into a brand, a corporate image in a way.'

On the back of these positive reviews and the rapid acceptance of the album by both new and dedicated fans, *Dark Side of the Moon* entered the US album chart at #42 on March 24, a week when the film soundtrack *Deliverance* was at number one. Over the next month it rose up the charts, hitting #27, #9, #6 and #3 before finally, on April 28, it knocked Alice Cooper's *Billion Dollar Babies* album off the top spot.

It held the number one position for just that one week before Elvis Presley's *Aloha From Hawaii Via Satellite* took over to be followed by Led Zeppelin's *Houses of the Holy*. And, after all the efforts they made to secure *Dark Side of the Moon* for America and ensure that it was a success, it was perhaps appropriate that the record company took out a full page advert in the US music trade press to shout about the news.

Placed in the May 5 1973 issues of Billboard, Cashbox and Record World, the advertisement seems to be another one that was designed by the US label's in-house art department rather than Floyd's approved Hipgnosis team as it carried six small square images – all in black and white – tracing the cover from a plain pyramid to the final cover image. The two lines of headline text said: 'A Superb Number One Gold Album/With A Superb New

Single Money' and then printed the band's US dates from June 15 to June 19.

Having given the album a major thumbs-up, Loyd Grossman was never going to be taken aback by the impact it made in America. 'I wasn't surprised by its success although no one could have predicted just how massive and enduring that success would be.' Citing the 'sheer musicianship' and 'classy production values', Grossman picks out one other plus point. 'One of its great strengths, which no one would have dared point out at the time of release as it was so un-hip to speak in such terms, is that it is full of good tunes.'

The album's chart topping success in America was quickly noted by two EMI employees in the UK who had been involved with the record from the time it was completed in February. 'Their success never surprised me', says Nick Mobbs who recalls having a wager with Martin Nelson as they were arranging for the master tapes to be rushed to the States. 'We had a bet about what number we thought it would get to in the US. I did write down number one and Martin wrote down something like 35. I don't remember if there was any money involved but I did get a nice glow.'

And it seems that Mobbs and Nelson were not the only people betting on the outcome of *Dark Side of the Moon* as there are reports that Dave Gilmour had a wager with manager Steve O'Rourke that the album would not even enter the US top 10.

As Capitol basked in the success of their campaign, EMI's Harvest division had their own plan for the album's release in Britain. It involved full pages adverts in the March 17 issue of each of the major music papers of the day – Melody Maker, New Musical Express, Sounds and Disc – which featured an 8cm square album cover set against a huge background shot of Egypt's famous pyramids.

In the same week's edition of the trade paper Music Week, the UK music industry was treated to a story which announced that

EMI were offering sale or return terms on four Harvest albums in a £20,000 campaign featuring *Dark Side of the Moon*, T Rex's *Tanx*, ELO's *ELO 2* and *Wizzard Brew* by Wizzard. The story also explained that even before the campaign had begun a total of over 100,000 copies of the four albums had been already been sold.

'Because they were Floyd there would have automatically been a campaign which involved full page music paper adverts,' says Nick Mobbs who also recalls another aspect of the promotional push. 'There was always the question of tour support – when the manager comes in and asks for a contribution to a tour - and I'm pretty sure we gave them some cash as they were touring in support of the album … something like £5,000 would have been reasonable back then.'

And while Harvest installed window displays and put up posters around the country, one ingredient was still missing from the campaign. 'By this stage they just weren't doing interviews. I think that by then they had created this aura, a sort of mystique, and having no publicity added to it,' suggests Mobbs. 'They also liked not being recognized and I was cool with that – they were selling records and you could only do this when you got that point.'

Even so he takes some satisfaction in persuading one member of the band to talk to one small publication, the EMI Records in-house magazine Music Talk. 'I did get Nick – and I still look back on it as an incredible success – do an interview with them and I told him it wasn't for the public but would be a big thing for people at EMI. He agreed to do it … in return for a lunch.'

Pink Floyd's disinterest in promoting their new album came as no surprise to Pete Jenner who had seen the band develop into a smaller and tighter community. 'They had a very closed little world which they lived in with few outsiders. I don't think they were particularly hostile to the record company – they were just indifferent.' He goes on, 'They weren't going to do what was required of them, the record company was a means to an end and they were not in control of the band.'

In the circumstances EMI were forced to come up with a clever and unusual marketing wheeze aimed directly at Floyd's core market. It involved Martin Nelson going on a tour of the UK with his EMI Ford Cortina stuffed with a sound system from Abbey Road. He recalls: 'I had two huge speakers, two quad amps and a twin desk which just about fitted into the back of the car and I went off on the road.' The plan was for him to go to universities and introduce students to the new Pink Floyd album.

'I went out on the road following tours by other bands and when they had finished I set up a Dark Side playback,' remembers Nelson. 'At Exeter University the Kinks drew around 1500 people and then I ended up with about 500 of them sat on the floor listening to Dark Side.' Throughout March and into April of 1973, Nelson went all over the country plugging the new album directly to the fans. 'I started off with a white label and I also arranged with university social secretaries to do lunch time playbacks.'

And after the students had sat and listened to the album in compete silence, the plan was that they went out and bought a copy and at the same time spread the word about Dark Side. 'There was no other way of getting the whole album played to people, and university students were a prime audience for Floyd and their new album,' explains Nelson.

For Roxy Music's Phil Manzanera, the fact that the members of Pink Floyd did not take part in any campaign to promote their album came as something of a surprise. 'I do remember people saying that there were no photos of Floyd anywhere. It was always sort of an anti-campaign and they did incredibly well for doing nothing to promote the album,' he says before reflecting on how and why it succeeded. 'The whole industry was a lot smaller then and word of mouth was important. I also think it appealed to a lot of stoned people as it had elements of chill out and ambient music about it for the people on drugs and that worked.'

When the album finally came out in the UK – on March 23 1973 – it made an immediate impact, even on those who were doubters. On seeing the completed cover artwork, photographer Gered Mankowitz was forced to admit that 'it turned out to be the absolutely perfect image for the album and full credit to all concerned.' At the same time the UK music press was busy getting to grips with the album, and in general they gave it the thumbs up.

For Melody Maker's Roy Hollingsworth the opening side was '… so utterly confused with itself that it was difficult to follow' but he considered side two to be 'fabulous' as 'the songs, the sounds, the rhythm were solid and sound.' Meanwhile Let It Rock magazine felt the album less impressive than the band's live performance of the music in 1972 but conceded that, 'It is still a fascinating record with moments of great power and a compelling atmosphere of melancholy and drama. But something has been lost. And as an afterthought they added, 'Unfortunately however he's [Waters] not the world's greatest songwriter.'

Over at NME Tony Stewart suggested, 'Musically this album is not unsimilar to the style formulated with first, *Atom Heart Mother* and then *Meddle*, though thematically it's stronger – on the most worldly of subjects: madness. With the possibility of sounding a little high faluting, Dark Side is about life and the result is not too pretty a picture, particularly as suggested by 'Eclipse'.' He concludes by saying, 'Probably this is Floyd's most successful artistic venture. Not only are the lyrics statements of opinion, usually quite discernable, but they're enhanced by some clever tape effects. And there are hideous mad-man laughs frequently recurring.'

It was left to Steve Peacock at Sounds to receive the album almost without reservation. 'This is the album that I think Pink Floyd have been working towards for years. It has all the hallmarks of the Floyd's best playing and writing – the fat chords, the utterly dependable anchor of the rhythm section, the slowly building dimensions, the understated but insistent style of the vocals and the finely judged explosion of guitars, keyboards or treated sound.' Peacock, who later worked for the BBC (he became the editor of Radio 4's Farming Today), concluded his review by saying: 'I don't care if you've never heard of the Floyd's music in your life, I unreservedly recommend everyone to *Dark Side of the Moon*.'

At the same time Floyd fan Paul Weller from Margate (not the future Jam singer from Surrey) wrote to Melody Maker's Readers Letters page to offer slightly begrudging congratulations to the band 'because the Floyd are showing very definite signs of changing their musical direction'.

DARK SIDE OF THE MOON REVEALED

Chapter Ten

In the weeks prior to the album's release in the UK, Pink Floyd journeyed to America to play a 16- date tour in support of this final release for Capitol Records. After opening in Wisconsin on March 4, the tour ended up in New York at the legendary Radio City Music Hall in mid-March and Capitol's Dan Davis remembers the occasion vividly. 'After the concert we went down to the reception area where we could tell the band how great they were – all the usual stuff. I was not a pot smoker but there was so much pot being smoked in that room at Radio City that you couldn't see across the room for smoke.'

Despite the 'meet and greet' in New York, the Capitol executive remains convinced that the band never wanted to build any sort of relationship. 'They did not make themselves terribly available to those of us at the record company', recounts Davis. 'Roger Waters came into the Tower once and he was anything but cordial towards us.'

Long time LA resident Peter Asher embraced the new album by his British compatriots and took it upon himself to do some promotion work on behalf of Floyd. 'I made sure all my engineer friends heard Dark Side and they all became huge fans,' says the three-time winner of the Grammy for Producer of the Year, who also readily admits to having his work as a producer influenced by the record. 'I couldn't point to a particular place and say I stole this idea from the Floyd but it certainly gave one licence to try virtually anything in terms of sound.'

The band's growing status in America - with both the music industry and the public - was further boosted by the leading US music publication Rolling Stone who were moved to describe Pink Floyd as 'experimenting with concept albums and pot-friendly studio effects and breaking free of conventional pop-song formats'.

However it was the UK press reviews for *Dark Side of the Moon* which alerted British record dealer Andy Gray to the imminent arrival of a new album. With thriving open-air businesses in Cambridge (Mondays to Fridays) and Bury St Edmunds (Saturdays), Gray became the first market stall holder to have an account with EMI Records and the association between Floyd and Cambridge made the new album a must-have title on his stalls. 'I had heard about the album in the music press but had never seen the band live although Syd Barrett used to come round to the stall in Cambridge after he left the group,' says Gray, who later ran Andy's Records, the UK's largest chain of independent record shops, with over 40 stores before its closure in 2003.

'The first real banging of the drum would have been when the EMI rep came round to take an order and me trying to predict how many I needed to order,' recalls Gray. Estimating that he may have pre-ordered as many as 1,000 copies, Gray does remember the day when they were delivered. 'I recall the guy turning up from WHSmith – they delivered the stock in those days – with loads of boxes of Dark Side and having them stacked up all around the back of the stall.'

When he sold his first delivery, Gray then ordered a second batch of album and they sold out just as quickly. 'Being in Cambridge was the perfect place because of the band's links and the huge student population', he says. 'At the time it was probably the biggest advance order I had ever placed for an album. I remember being surrounded by boxes and boxes of *Dark Side of the Moon* ... and then getting a huge bill from EMI.'

When *Dark Side of the Moon* came out Nick Turnbull was working in the stockroom at HMV's flagship store in the West End of London and in addition to buying a copy for himself, he recalls that there was a steady trade for the new release. 'It continually sold well but not in massive quantities and I remember we had a window display for the album but there was no further promotion.'

As a Floyd fan, Turnbull was in a good position to assess the band's appeal in 1973. 'They had been around for a number of years, steadily growing their fanbase and then *Meddle* was released and that sold well even though the sleeve was worse for identification than Dark Side.' In fact he was such a fan that he saw the band perform music from Dark Side twice during 1972 and even treated himself to a copy of the 'Tour 72' bootleg album.

Being on the staff in Britain's major record store, which was opened at 363 Oxford Street in 1921 and was in fact owned by Floyd's record company EMI until the mid-nineties, Turnbull was able to identify the type of people who came into the store to buy *Dark Side of the Moon*. 'While the student aspect was important, Pink Floyd weren't playing colleges anymore. They were playing to more affluent audiences who had their friends round to have a few beers, get stoned and listen to some music. They then went out and bought the album, had some more friends round to have a few beers and get stoned ... and listen to the album.'

For radio and TV presenter Bob Harris, receiving a copy of the album made 'a massive impression' and he recalls that the finished copy represented a long period of effort. 'Some of the threads leading up to Dark Side had been developing over the year', explains the host of BBC Radio's *In Concert* and *Sounds of the Seventies*, and of TV's *The Old Grey Whistle Test*. 'It did break new ground particularly when you look at the layers. They were pushing out the technological barriers and testing everything in a massive way,' he says. 'It wasn't a happy album and the spoken word element just adds an atmosphere and, at certain times, a sense of menace to the philosophical flavour they wanted to create.'

Harris, who still presents shows on BBC Radio 2, was also taken with the album's presentation. 'Visually it all seemed to make sense – very bold, very specific and there was nothing else on the racks that looked like that with the absolutely black cover and the colours of the rainbow; it really was striking.'

With Pink Floyd issuing no singles from their new album, it was left to late-night radio shows like Harris's *Sounds of the Seventies* to feature tracks from it ,and both Harris and his producer Jeff Griffin placed great emphasis on the show's independence – and its non-reliance on the Radio 1 daytime play list – to be able to programme Dark Side.

'We had complete freedom and that was something that I personally valued at the time', says Griffin while Harris adds, 'We could play whatever we liked – and turn the volume up really loud in the studio. The programme was there specifically to be a vehicle for the experimental at a time when the album market was particularly vigorous.'

For Harris, a co-founder of Time Out magazine in 1968 in offices shared with Floyd's original management company Blackhill – 'I remember seeing Syd slumped in a chair in reception' - the difference between *Sounds of the Seventies* and the daily 'strip' shows on Radio 1 was summed up by a long-time Radio 1 producer who eventually became the station's Controller. 'Johnny Beerling coined the phrase 'ratings by day and reputations by night', and that was a really good way of putting it.'

So with Pink Floyd clearly falling into the 'reputations by night' category, it was down to the specialist radio and TV shows to promote Britain's new swathe of progressive rock bands in general, and *Dark Side of the Moon* in particular. With no play on the most popular day time radios shows -   hosted by the likes of Dave Lee Travis, Tony Blackburn and Noel Edmonds – BBC2's *The Old Grey Whistle Test* was the obvious vehicle for the new album, but there was one major problem: Floyd were not prepared to play live.

'Basically they could not reproduce their music in our studio', says Harris, recalling that in the early days the OGWT studio only had around eight microphone points. 'And the six-day set-up period would have been a problem. At that time there were certain bands – Floyd, Yes, ELO and Genesis – when you realised that the complexity of what they were doing was too much for the technology available at the BBC.'

Bizarrely, however, OGWT seems to have given a second airing to Ian Emes' film set to 'One of These Days' from the earlier *Meddle* album in April 1973 – just a week after Dark Side was released – rather than attempt to create a film of their own to go with a track from the new album.

Within a week of its release *Dark Side of the Moon* entered the UK charts on March 31 at number two. It was kept off the top spot by a TV-advertised K-Tel compilation entitled *20 Flashback Great Hits Of The Sixties* and within a week had dropped down to number five, as Led Zeppelin and The Faces went to number one during the following month.

One man who became aware of Dark Side almost from the outset was Tim Rice although the award- winning lyricist readily admits that 'prog rock' was not his music of choice. 'Maybe I was too old for it and was more into Californian music', he says but his fascination with all things related to the pop charts meant he could not ignore it. 'I'm sure I bought the album fairly early in its life but probably in anorak mode rather than anything else – it was doing quite well so I thought I had better have one.'

There was, however, one other element about the album which intrigued Rice – the appearance of backing singer Clare Torry. 'I knew Clare from my early days as an assistant at Abbey Road when she sent me a tape in around 1966. I thought she was really good and remember telling producer Norrie Paramor [he had made hit records for Helen Shapiro, Cliff Richard and The Shadows] that she was somebody we should keep an eye on. I often tell her that I discovered her.'

While admitting that he didn't foresee the album's success – 'I didn't for one moment think it was going to be one of the great albums of all time' – Rice was impressed by two numbers in particular. 'I thought Clare's performance on 'The Great Gig in the Sky' was phenomenal – one of her great triumphs – and 'Money' was the track that was played in those days.' In fact the popularity of Waters' six minute-plus song with its sound effects of loose change and a cash register was such that Capitol in America had a plan to use the track to further sales of Dark Side.

According to Rupert Perry, it was all down to Capitol's head of promotion Al Coury who insisted that in order to 'drive the album on' they needed to issue a single. This was, however, easier said than done and it was down to Bhaskar Menon to once again negotiate with Steve O'Rourke. After the album's initial burst of success in America, it was clear to Capitol's president that a second phase was necessary. 'It took a considerable amount of persuasion, they needed a lot of convincing,' says Menon before explaining that 'the catalyst that would quickly propel it on to the next kind of audience' was America's all-important Top 40 AM radio.

While he recalls that there was some debate about which track to release as a single, Don Zimmermann reflects that radio made the choice easier: 'The stations were all over 'Money' and we knew that concentrated Top 40 airplay could make the difference between a hit and a mega smash.' Described as accessible, commercial and, by Menon as 'an almost self-evident choice', an edited version of 'Money' was released in America on May 7 1973 with 'Any Colour You Like' as the B-side.

Cited as probably the only record in 7/4 time to enter the US Top 20 – and also featuring what has been dubbed as 'one of the most memorable classic bass riffs ever recorded' – 'Money' was edited down to 3 minutes and 59 seconds from the full length 6.20 seconds album version for release as a single, but the first decision involved whether or not to include the word 'bullshit' from the original album track.

It was decided that the promo single would be released to radio with a mono side excluding the word while the stereo side featured the uncensored word 'bullshit'. This was subsequently replaced by a new promo version of the single which featured a censored version on both sides and carried an advisory note from the record company: 'Please disregard the previous Pink Floyd single which you have received. This is the correct Pink Floyd promo single with the word bulls—t edited on both the mono and stereo sides. From the LP The *Dark Side of the Moon*, a certified million seller and #1 album in the country.'

In their weekly round up of the new single releases, Billboard linked 'Money' and Deep Purple's 'Fire on the Water' together for commentary and declared that both bands had experienced 'rough going with singles' despite their album success before commenting, 'Now we have them being accepted by AM programmers.'

On May 19, 'Money' entered the US singles chart at #84, by the end of June it was at #26 and, after 11 weeks on the chart, it peaked at #13 on July 28, while Jim Croce, Billy Preston and The Carpenters were in the top five. Interestingly two weeks later Deep Purple's 'Fire on the Water' hit the number four spot.

Two Floyd members offered up their view on the release of their first single for over four years. Mason explained, 'We decided that if the public didn't want to buy our singles we didn't want to put any out' while Wright concluded, 'We didn't think anything would happen with 'Money'. And suddenly it just did.' Guitarist Gilmour also recalled that the single's success had an effect on their live performances. 'Everywhere we played, we suddenly found ourselves confronted with an audience that just wanted to hear the big hit. That's all you'd hear throughout the show until we finally played it – "Money' ... play 'Money"'.

Music fan Loyd Grossman remembers the impact the single made in America. "Money' did get played quite a lot', he says. 'It was a time when US radio stations were prepared to give more airtime to what was then rather quaintly called 'underground' music and, as the most commercial sounding track on Dark Side, it drew attention to the album.'

'Money' was Floyd's first single release since the unsuccessful 'Point Me at the Sky' in December 1968 and Pete Jenner believes that the track 'was one of the key things – it was so witty' but he is still surprised it was taken off of the album for release. 'Normally they wouldn't put out a single but perhaps Capitol said 'We've given you half a million, now give us a single'. I suspect it was probably over Roger's dead body.' But even with its success in the US, there was little likelihood of a single ever seeing the light of day in the UK.

'There was never any discussion about doing a single in the UK,' confirms Harvest chief Nick Mobbs whose stance was similar to the one Jenner suggested for Waters. 'It would have been over my dead body. I never dreamt of having a single and they were so well-known by then that it wasn't even considered.'

However, the commercial success of 'Money' did make an impact on the band according to Gilmour. Having declared that before Dark Side the band was seen as 'some form of intellectual rock n roll', he announced, 'It was 'Money' that made the difference rather than *Dark Side of the Moon*. It gave us a much larger following for which we should be thankful.'

And it wasn't just in America that 'Money' did the job for Floyd, as Angola, Australia, Austria, Belgium, Canada, Denmark, France, Germany, Greece, Italy, Mexico, Netherlands, New Zealand, Norway, Portugal and Spain all issued the single with the B-side of 'Any Colour You Like'. Bolivia went out on a limb and coupled it with 'Speak to Me', and Mexico opted to re-release it in the same year with 'Us and Them' as a B-side.

While *Dark Side of the Moon* became a permanent fixture in the album charts on both sides of the Atlantic, it was also making an impression all around the world. Number one in the charts in Belgium, Canada, France and New Zealand, it also went top ten in Australia, Austria, Brazil, Finland, Germany, Holland, Italy, Norway and Spain.

Reflecting years later on the success of Dark Side, Joe Boyd, the man who produced the group's first ever single, said 'None of us imagined that decades later you could go to the remotest parts of the globe and find cassettes of *Dark Side of the Moon* rattling around the glove compartments of third-world taxis along with Madonna and Michael Jackson.'

The album also earned engineer Alan Parsons a 1974 Grammy nomination for Best Engineered Album – Non Classical although he (and Dark Side) lost out to Malcolm Cecil and Robert Margouleff for their work on Stevie Wonder's album *Innervisions*.

However, according to Capitol boss Bhaskar Menon, the success of their global best seller was not something the band needed to either acknowledge or discuss. 'The sales figures and the marketing power spoke for themselves – what really remained to be discussed?' he says. Harvest chief Nick Mobbs also recalls a general reluctance to talk about or celebrate their hit. 'I can't think that I ever had a conversation with the band about their success – it was something that would never have arisen'

In fact at least one band member made his feelings very clear about any gold and platinum discs they might receive. 'I remember Roger saying something about not wanting to be part of any presentation. He was vehemently against presentations of any kind,' recalls Mobbs whose reaction was to play a prank on the band's bass player. 'As a joke I got his gold discs and wrapped them up in the grottiest brown paper we could find and had them delivered to his house.'

After Mobbs had sent Waters his presentation sales discs in the 'grottiest brown paper', the Harvest label chief found himself on the receiving end of Floyd's generosity albeit with an odd twist. When news of his impending marriage leaked out, they were asked by the band what they wanted as a wedding present. However, when the bridegroom told Floyd what they wanted he was in for a surprise.

'When I said that we needed a washing machine, the word came back that they wouldn't buy us a washing machine and a hi-fi system was suggested instead,' says Mobbs. 'And when it arrived in loads of boxes there was a card signed 'from Nick and Steve' (Mason and O'Rourke)and I don't know whether that was a pointed gesture to suggest that the others didn't want to sign it or that they weren't around.'

Chapter Eleven

With the album now firmly fixed in both the UK and US charts, Floyd put together two major London shows in advance of an America tour and then retained Handsworth-born Birmingham filmmaker Ian Emes, to work with their new album.

'They commissioned me in 1973 to do a sequence for the song 'Time' from the finished tracks they sent me,' recalls Emes. 'I was given carte blanche and complete freedom to interpret as I thought best. It was a case of breaking it all down and then doing storyboards.'

While it's difficult to pin down exactly when Emes' accompanying film for 'Time' was actually broadcast on Old Grey Whistle Test, producer Mike Appleton remembers being approached about a new film. 'I remember someone saying that, as this new animation came about as a result of the association created between Floyd and Ian - after OGWT transmitted French Windows – we might be interested in showing it. It came either directly from the band or somebody in EMI's promotion department.'

DARK SIDE OF THE MOON REVEALED

According to host Bob Harris the film was 'a Godsend' and the fact that OGWT was one of the few TV shows prepared to run Emes' Floyd films added to the show's reputation. 'There was a sense that we had discovered this, there was a sense of exclusivity because you either saw the film at a Floyd show or on OGWT – nobody else was showing it.'

While the then 24 year-old Emes admits 40 years on that 'I never knew that it was shown on Old Grey Whistle Test', he knows he was in the audience at Earls Court in May 1973 to see his work become an integral part of Floyd's new live extravaganza. 'I was aware of the exhilaration of sitting in the front row and seeing my work on an enormous screen, he says. 'Nothing beats that – my work having that kind of effect on that many people. Just seeing rows of long-haired people with my clocks flying all over them and thinking, 'Bloody hell.''

Also in the audience for one of the Earls Court shows was Chris Thomas, who recalls that it was as a result of asking Floyd's manager for a favour. 'I asked Steve O'Rourke for six tickers because Roxy Music wanted to go and they knew I had worked on the album.' But when he got the tickets – which he thinks were at least free – Thomas was in for a shock. 'They were at the furthest end of Earls Court – right at the back, as far away from the stage as you could be.' And he was then faced with another problem:

'Roxy Music were all in their quite glittery, glammy outfits sitting at the very back of the hall saying to me 'Do you really know the band?'.I couldn't believe Steve had given me such awful seats.' Thomas had to think quickly to appease the rising young stars from Roxy Music, who were celebrating For Your Pleasure becoming their first top five album. 'It was so embarrassing but I explained to the band that the wonderful thing about Floyd is that you didn't have to be close to the stage, that the show is 'the thing' so the seats we had were the best you could get to watch the show from.'

While Thomas was cringing in the back row watching Floyd, Alan Parsons, credited as engineer on Dark Side, was working on the desk as sound engineer in the cavernous 19,000 capacity Earls Court arena just ahead of a major job opportunity. 'Pink Floyd offered me a salaried job to do all their recording and sound work and I would have been involved in setting up Britannia Row but it was at a time when I was involved with Pilot and Cockney Rebel so I said no and that I was going to continue with my production career.'

(* Britannia Row was the studio Pink Floyd built and opened in Islington, North London in the mid 1970s and where they recorded Animals and The Wall. Eventually, drummer Nick Mason took over sole ownership before selling it in the 1990s.)

Looking back on the offer, Parsons says reluctantly that it would have been 'a dead end job and my entire life would have become Pink Floyd' but still acknowledges that he has 'more positive than negative memories of Dark Side'. The producer – and one time head of Abbey Road Studios – recalls that he recommended a young English producer to Floyd at that time. 'I suggested they give the job to James Guthrie,' he says before explaining that Guthrie's later involvement in various remixed and re-mastered versions of Dark Side of the Moon led to further issues. 'I was really pissed off with him when he mixed the surround version without contacting me – another reason for my frustrations with Floyd.'

Having toured America in March 1973, Floyd returned to the States in June for 13 shows including a record breaking appearance at New Jersey's Roosevelt Stadium when they grossed over $110,000 for a single performance. By the end of 1973, the band had racked up a total of 98 dates across the UK, Europe, Japan and North America in support of Dark Side of the Moon.

Floyd's success in America – the album remained in the top three of the US album chart from the end of July through to September

1973 – was a major boost for both the performance and reputation of Capitol Records as Rupert Perry confirms. 'It was important that Capitol was seen as a company that could deliver. We had Grand Funk Railroad but Capitol's roster was pretty thin and that was another reason why it was important to get this album and prove that we could deliver.'

And, according to Perry, the impact made by *Dark Side of the Moon* was immediate. 'It made things a lot easier in A&R as we could point to what we had done with Floyd. One the back of Dark Side we were able to resurrect Capitol Records in a lot of ways.' Talking to the British corporation's in-house newspaper EMI News in September 1973, Bhaskar Menon, Capitol's president explained his company's philosophy. 'When the artist is in central focus you must continue to bolster acceptance, keep close to everything he is doing. Take Pink Floyd. They are one of the world's most talented groups who were not a success in the United States. Until now.'

In fact the company's figures for the first half year of 1973 showed the importance of *Dark Side of the Moon* to Capitol's recovery. The label reported net income of $5,232,000, a massive 276% increase compared to the six months to June 1972 with Floyd lining up on the best sellers list alongside Grand Funk, Helen Reddy, the Steve Miller Band, Anne Murray, The Band and assorted solo releases from George Harrison, Paul McCartney, John Lennon and Ringo Starr.

But, despite Capitol's best efforts, there was little or no chance of Floyd remaining with the label. Rick Wright explained the reasons behind their move to CBS by saying, 'We thought they would be best for us largely because of their size. They were well organised. When we left Capitol they were badly organized.' Bhaskar Menon confirms that Capitol were fighting a lost cause. 'Steve O'Rourke asked me a couple of times informally whether we would be willing to match the CBS terms if he could extricate the band from the CBS deal.'

While stressing that it would have been improper to discuss or proffer any deal which could be considered as interference with the group's commitment fore the future with CBS, Menon did tell O'Rourke that if he could 'peaceably' get out of the CBS deal then Capitol would be available to talk terms. 'But that could only be after the CBS deal in North America was mutually terminated and without even the slightest risk of 'interference' with that deal.'

Although, according to Perry, Floyd's manager 'did not want the momentum of Dark Side to stop', Pink Floyd were locked into a new deal with a new record company. The president of Columbia Records was Clive Davis and he first got interested in signing Pink Floyd long before *Dark Side of the Moon*. 'Towards the end of 1971 and during 1972 I kept hearing great word of mouth about Pink Floyd,' he remarked in his 1974 book Inside The Record Business.

He also reflected on the group's situation in America at that time. 'Once again it was a case of a group being unhappy – this time on Capitol. They were not selling what they thought they should. Their concerts were sellouts; their record sales didn't reflect it.' Through a colleague, Davis extended an invitation to manager Steve O'Rourke to attend his company's weekly singles meeting. 'It worked like a charm. Columbia was what he wanted and he agreed to come if the terms were right.'

Although the terms have never been made public – it was reported as a $1 million deal – Davis did give away a few details of his negotiations. 'It was the end of 1972: the contract would take effect at the beginning of 1974 and the group wanted about two hundred and fifty thousand dollars advanced on signing.' While he admitted that most of the business advisors at Columbia were against the deal because of the time lag and up-front advance, Davis reflected on the success of their final Capitol album. '*Dark Side of the Moon* album sold over two million copies and stayed around the top of the best selling albums charts well into 1974. This was a giant acquisition.'

Floyd's decision to move across country and sign to the New York-based CBS Records for America took the band back to a label with the same name as the one they had started out on in the UK in 1967. The original Columbia label had been formed in North America in 1887 and bought by CBS in 1938, seven years after its British affiliate the Columbia Graphophone Company had merged with the established Gramophone Company to form EMI. The British market leaders then continued to operate a Columbia label, boasting Cliff Richard, the Animals, Dave Clark Five, Gerry & the Pacemakers and (briefly) Pink Floyd, until the early 1990s when the rights to Columbia in the UK and in an assortment of international territories were purchased by Sony who had bought CBS Records in 1987.

Despite his grand words and the kudos he got from acquiring Pink Floyd from under the noses of Capitol, Clive Davis didn't stay at Columbia long enough to see them issue any new albums. In May 1973 – just a few months after signing the group he was fired by CBS amid allegations of financial discrepancies and shortly after Capitol executive Perry remembers speaking with Floyd's manager. 'Steve O'Rourke said he didn't know anyone to deal with at CBS after Clive had gone. He told me that he was on holiday in the Caribbean early in 1974 when he got a visit from a key CBS player and it turned out to be a very smartly dressed Walter Yetnikoff.'

American lawyer Yetnikoff had joined CBS as a lawyer in 1961 – recruited by Davis from the same private law firm where they both began their careers – and in 1975 he was named as President of the CBS Records Group.

Chapter Twelve

Before the end of 1973 Capitol attempted to further drive the sales of *Dark Side of the Moon* by delivering to radio a promotional EP containing the tracks 'Time', 'Breathe', 'Us and Them' and 'Money', which they followed with a commercial single release featuring just 'Time' and 'Us and Them' in February 1974.

While it staggered to #101 in the US and failed to make any impression in Canada, the track 'Time' was coupled with 'Breathe' in France and with 'Money' in Thailand. While these records were issued for sale they were primarily part of the campaign to keep Dark Side in the public consciousness and in the charts.

Ahead of the singles, January 1974 saw the re-release of the band's first two albums – The *Piper at the Gates of Dawn* and *A Saucerful of Secrets* – in a package entitled somewhat dubiously *A Nice Pair.* It peaked at #21 in the UK and managed a top 40 place – at #36 – in the US chart. A few months later, ex-band member Syd Barrett's first two albums *The Madcap Laughs* and *Barrett* were similarly packaged together under the banner *Syd Barrett,* but failed to chart on either side of the Atlantic.

More recognition of Floyd's success with Dark Side came in the shape of the music papers' annual polls. NME ran a championship based on points awarded for chart positions and the 1973 league saw Floyd as runners up followed by a number four placing the following year. By the end of 1974, the band and their record label were able to assemble all the *Dark Side of the Moon* awards into one advert which they placed in each of Britain's music papers.

Under a photograph of the Pink Floyd football team – which included all four band members – the copy read: '*Dark Side of the Moon* No 1 album – NME Readers Poll 1974 British section World section; MM Readers Pop Poll 1973 British Section International Section; Sounds Readers Poll 1974 British Section International Section; Disc Top Albums 1973; MM Top Albums 1973. And they finished off with a pay off line for the new *A Nice Pair* album.

While America's Creem magazine listed Dark Side at number six in its readers poll of top albums of 1973 and 'Money' as the eighth best single, Floyd again featured in NME's 1975 Poll when they were voted #2 Best British Group (behind Manzanera's Roxy Music), #2 Best British Stage Band (behind Genesis), #5 Best World Group and then strangely #1 Best World Stage Band – best in the world but not best in Britain!

But there were still no interviews or any other promotional activities involving the band during 1974 although Gilmour, Mason, Waters and Wright did eventually turn their attention to the question of the follow up album to Dark Side. After dates in France and ahead of a winter tour of the UK, work began on an idea that was so extraordinary and laborious that it remains to this day an uncompleted piece of either genius or madness.

Harvest manager Nick Mobbs was unconcerned about a follow up – 'I was happy for them to work Dark Side for two years by playing it live' he explains – and he certainly wasn't about to badger his top band with any requests. 'I never pressed them about a follow-up and was happy to do what they wanted. I was not the EMI man who said 'We've sold 300,000 units boys, we need another one by September'.'

However, despite EMI's relaxed attitude – no doubt reinforced by the continuing success of Dark Side – Floyd returned to Abbey Road in 1974 to embark on a project entitled 'Household Objects' which Mason once explained was a 'brilliant device to postpone having to create anything concrete for the foreseeable future … we could busy ourselves with the mechanics of the sounds rather than the creation of music.'

Comparing themselves to an 'adult playgroup', the band used broken light bulbs, wine glasses, egg slicers, broom bristles, rubber bands, sticky tape and bowls of water in their efforts to make 'Household Objects'. 'We using anything we could use,' said Gilmour back in 1988. 'And actually a rubber band over a plank of wood does make a fantastic bass note but it was a very, very long arduous process and we suddenly went 'why?' Why on earth were we bothering to do this the difficult way when we could make all the noises much easier with musical instruments?'

Acknowledging that 'in those days technology was nowhere what it is today with sampling', Gilmour pronounced the whole thing 'virtually impossible' while Abbey Road engineer Parsons was 'disappointed that it never came to anything.' Drummer Mason also confirmed that 'progress was negligible' and eventually, with the band unable to pretend any longer that they were actually doing anything genuinely musical, he confirmed that 'the whole project was gently laid to rest'.

With no real follow up to Dark Side on the horizon, Floyd embarked on a 20-date UK tour in late 1974, beginning on November 4 in Edinburgh's Usher Hall, and ending at the Hippodrome, Bristol, which included four nights at London's Empire

Pool in Wembley. A regular visitor to the backstage area during the tour was Harvest's Nick Mobbs, and he recalls that relaxing with a post-show celebration was not Floyd's way. 'After a show they analysed everything and never wanted people to come back and say 'great gig' when they knew it hadn't been. They were always hyper-critical of their performances and knew when even the smallest things had gone wrong.'

One of the more intricate and complicated new additions to their stage set was a circular projection screen and this represented an new opportunity for 'Time' filmmaker Ian Emes. Now he was charged with producing more new animated footage for use on the latest tour.

Fortunately he never considered Floyd's Dark Side album to be in any way desperate. 'It's releasing and as an animator I responded to Floyd's work without realising it, as a spatial experience,' says Emes. The more he listened to their music and worked with the four band members, the more he understood. 'I knew Rick was a classically trained musician and then you had Nick's driving rhythms. You had Roger's kind of big landscape sensibility, and then the harmonizing effect of Dave – and between Dave and Roger you got this frisson, this balance.'

He also came to understand who was responsible for what on the band's Dark Side album. 'Roger was the scary stuff which I loved but Dave brought it back to a more human level. You had tenderness and aggressiveness and the whole range of human emotions but at the same time you had a big landscape in the experience.' As a man who by his own admission deals in 'space visually', Emes was determined to create films which did justice to Floyd's music and that involved working long hours to meet the band's tour deadlines.

'I had story-boarded four times more than I was able to achieve in the time – people didn't really understand how long animation took in those days,' he recalls. In an effort to bring everything in on time, he 'scaled up' from the one-man operation that had made French Windows in six months to employing 30 people to work on the sequences for *Dark Side of the Moon*.

'It was a block of two months from July 1974,' says Emes, 'and I was having to produce 20 to 30 minutes of animated film, which would normally take six months. I worked around the clock to get enough material ready in time for the tour and then they commissioned live film of 'Money' and 'Us and Them' as well.' And all the time, the band were waiting and watching to see what Emes produced.

'Roger was very vocal about everything — about what it felt like,' recalls the film producer. 'I was OK with that although it felt a bit like an art college crit for me – 'things to improve, things to bring out' – but not all in a destructive way. Roger was the main commentator and it was positive artistic comment in the main.'

Emes' film work was not the only 'special' visual effect to greet Floyd's fans on the tour. The tour programme appeared as a comic with band drawings by leading satirical cartoonist Gerald Scarfe and cartoon strips depicting the alter egos of each of the band members – Rog of the Rovers, Captain Mason R.N., Rich Right and Dave Derring.

As Pink Floyd moved on from *Dark Side of the Moon* and presumably put 'Household Objects' to the back of their minds, David Gilmour choose to speak to the New Musical Express in January 1975 when he admitted that in terms of musical virtuosity 'we're not really anywhere, individual musicianship is well below par.' While he took time out to deny that the band was 'bereft of ideas … just resting', the guitarist did acknowledge that *Dark Side of the Moon* 'trapped us creatively'.

After confirming a few years later that 'after Dark Side we were really floundering', Gilmour went further and in an interview with the author of this book outlined the thought processes behind the long awaited and much anticipated follow-up to their multi-million selling global phenomenon. 'Before *Dark Side of the Moon* the albums tended to be largely musical and not so much lyrics but *Dark Side of the Moon* was an opposite when the lyrics meant everything and for me it is weak in parts.'

Talking frankly in 1981 on the eve of Abbey Road's 50th anniversary as a studio, Gilmour admitted, 'We tried to fit the songs around the lyrics so sometimes the vehicle for a song was a little weak. What I certainly recognised and hustled the rest of the band to do, was to try and achieve a better balance.'

With that thought in mind and with Dark Side still firmly settled in both the UK and US charts, Floyd returned to Abbey Road in January 1975 to work on an album that would emerge nine months later as *Wish You Were Here*. And it arrived with a little bit of the madness from the aborted 'Household Objects' project intact. 'We actually did get some things off it which we used on *Wish You Were Here*,' says Gilmour citing the wine glasses that were used at the start of the album's opening track 'Shine On You Crazy Diamond'.

After recording had been interrupted for a tour of America and a headlining appearance at Britain's Knebworth festival – which featured a real spitfire and quadraphonic sound – Floyd ventured back into Abbey Road to complete their new album, and the song 'Shine On You Crazy Diamond' featured on the recording sheet.

Both the song and the summertime session were part of a slightly bizarre event that took place at Abbey Road when, during the recording of the album and part of 'Shine On You Crazy Diamond', an overweight Syd Barrett, complete with shaven head, wandered into the studio unrecognized as Floyd continued to make their music, and even asked if there was anything he could do to help out.

However, even though Shine On You Crazy Diamond was a tribute to the band's former founding member, Gilmour refused to be fazed by this strange turn of events. 'He turned up in the middle of the album but it was not surprising as he had often popped in unannounced over the years' while Waters confirmed that 'Shine On...' was 'about Syd because he had re-emerged at that point and had started coming to sessions again.'

One man who remembers the *Wish You Were Here* sessions for another reason is designer Aubrey Powell who spoke with the band's manager Steve O'Rourke around the time the new album was being recorded. 'I remember going to Steve and saying that we were vastly underpaid for the work on *Dark Side of the Moon*. He talked to the band who were all very grumpy about it because they thought we had already been paid,' explains Powell. 'I think we got around £2,000 probably from EMI and then they (Floyd) gave us another £5,000 which was quite a lot of money in the seventies.'

Having joined Harvest in 1974 as a radio and TV plugger working on Deep Purple, Mark Rye had moved up to be joint label manager by the time *Wish You Were Here* began to take shape. One of two men who took over from Nick Mobbs when he was put in charge of A&R for EMI Records, Rye readily admits that he had absolutely nothing to do with *Dark Side of the Moon*. 'It just kept going. You were running the label but you had no dealings with this band who produced this hugely successful album which was on your label.'

What Rye and his co-label manager Stuart Watson had to deal with was the dilemma of how to follow Dark Side. 'I remember going down to the studio and trying to get know the band but it was all very much 'How the fuck do you follow Dark Side?'' And the idea of using any of the success of Dark Side as a marketing tool in the campaign for the new album disappeared from the record company agenda pretty quickly. 'I recall that when we did *Wish You Were Here* we weren't allowed to cash in on Dark Side,' says Rye, 'it was to be very much a low-key campaign with no mention of Dark Side's success anywhere and once again they weren't going to turn up to press launches or anything else.'

Although he only ever met the band in the studio – they were still reluctant to visit the company's offices in Manchester Square – Rye sensed that they were in the throes of a change. 'They were still trying to come to terms with this huge album that they had released two years earlier. Throughout the *Wish You Were Here* period there was almost a complete avoidance of Dark Side. It was the elephant in the room – they didn't know to follow it, they didn't know what to do next.'

Chapter Thirteen

But somehow Pink Floyd had to follow *Dark Side of the Moon* and eventually they did it with *Wish You Were Here* which went straight to number one in America on October 4 1975, replacing Janis Ian's *Between the Lines* and holding on to the top spot for two weeks before being toppled by John Denver and his album *Windsong*. Still in the top three by November, *Wish You Were Here* was an almost instant platinum million-seller and also gave Columbia their first success with the band they had signed over a year earlier.

In the same week that *Wish You Were Here* reached number one in America, the album knocked Rod Stewart's *Atlantic Crossing* off the number one spot in the UK, but a week later Stewart had reclaimed the prime position. While it stayed in the US Top 40 for 15 weeks and in the UK top 75 for 90 weeks, band member Waters was apparently still less than impressed. 'The name [Pink Floyd] is probably worth one million sales of an album, any album we put out. Even if we just coughed, a million people will have ordered it simply because of the name.'

Comparing *Wish You Were Here* with Dark Side, Gilmour once told me, 'It works pretty well for me although it is not quite such a brilliant concept as *Dark Side of the Moon* but the highlights musically are higher than the musical highlights on *Dark Side of the Moon*.'

The recording of *Wish You Were Here* signalled the end of Floyd's long eight-year association with Abbey Road Studios which had begun with the making of 'Interstellar Overdrive' in March 1967. With the creation of their own Britannia Row studios, the band were free to spend their own time in their own studio without any of the potential corporate restrictions and confrontations.

For Gilmour, Abbey Road represented a perfectly acceptable studio that did its job well. 'Abbey Road was always fine with me but you can get great things out of any studio,' he once explained. 'The studios at Abbey Road for the most part have been up to date with the state of the art of the moment more or less', he said before adding, 'They tend to slip behind a bit sometimes because they are a bit bureaucratic.'

Out of Abbey Road and in Britannia Row, Pink Floyd started work on the follow-up to *Wish You Were Here* in April 1976, and once again Waters was at the forefront of the band's creativity as he emerged with his take on the grand Orwellian theme of likening humans to animals. He had written a song called 'Pigs' and then set about creating four more songs: 'Dogs' (written with Gilmour), 'Sheep' plus two further Pigs tracks, subtitled 'Three Different Ones' and 'On the Wing 2'.

While *Animals* failed to make number one either in Britain or America – it was number two in the UK and number three in the US – it has a place in rock history as the first album cover to cause a genuine threat to aviation. The idea was to suspend a giant inflatable pig from the four chimney stacks of London's iconic Battersea Power Station and photograph it to give the impression of the animal actually flying over the power station.

142

However things did not go to plan as the late Bob Mercer, former head of EMI Records UK recalled. 'Steve O'Rourke called and asked me to go down to the shoot which I wouldn't normally do, but as it was Floyd – and I had got to know the guys in the band who were always pretty remote from EMI – I told him I would go.'

Events on that December day in 1976 didn't go well for Mercer either as he got embroiled in a row about the Sex Pistols and their alleged bad behaviour in a hotel in Leeds, and when O'Rourke called late in the day to see why Mercer had not turned up, the EMI executive was told by the band's manager that Floyd's carefully planned album shoot had been a 'bloody mess, the pig escaped.'

Then as we all prepared to go home at the end of the day, the author in his capacity as head of press took a call from the chief of the British Airports Authority who wanted to talk to Mercer. 'He said he thought of me after they had to divert three planes from Paris to Gatwick,' remembered Mercer, 'as each of the pilots, flying at around 10,000 feet, reported seeing a pink pig in the sky. He said that it sounded like rock n roll to him and hence the call to me.' While Mercer called EMI France to alert them that the pig was heading in their direction, it apparently came down in a farm in Sussex much to the annoyance of a local farmer. 'He spent the next ten years suing Pink Floyd because he said that the pig had scared his cows into being milk-less – apparently he could get no milk from his dairy herd.'

The cover shot with a pig flying over Battersea was in fact an idea dreamt up by Waters who seemed to view the pig as a 'symbol of hope' but none of the photographs taken were considered suitable for the album cover so Hipgnosis dropped a picture of the pig onto one of the power station and mocked it up – in the days before computers.

Despite the involvement of Hipgnosis, Waters credited himself with the sleeve design and according to Powell it signalled a change in the relationship between the designers and the rock band. 'We never really had any fallings out until Animals when Roger asked me to do it without Storm', he says before commenting on the role the band's manager played in the situation: 'Steve O'Rourke was quite clever – he took a step back and let everybody get on with it and fight it out.'

The row resulted in Thorgerson and Hipgnosis not being involved with Floyd's sleeve designs for the next decade and it seems that this wasn't the only issue for Pink Floyd. Stories appeared in early 1977 which suggested all was not well within the band, as Mason admitted that the pressure of following both Dark Side and *Wish You Were Here* almost broke the band. 'I really did find the time in the studio extremely horrible,' he said, while Waters added that he found the last tour 'very unpleasant, un-nerving and upsetting.'

In fact it was reported that as the band's *Animals* tour came to an end in Canada in July 1977 was when Waters first came up with the idea of separating the band from the audience. Irritated by a noisy fan in the audience at Montreal's Olympic Stadium, Waters was alleged to have spat at him and decided that building a wall might be the answer to keep the fans at bay.

But, despite these problems, they soldiered on, although in the two and half years between *Animals* and Floyd's next studio effort, various members of the band amused themselves with a series of solo projects. After producing Robert Wyatt's critically acclaimed *Rock Bottom* album in 1974, Mason performed similar duties for The Damned's *Music For Pleasure* and co-produced Steve Hillage's *Green* album in 1978. Meanwhile, Wright recorded his solo album of 1978, *Wet Dream*. At the same time Gilmour issued his eponymous debut solo album and busied himself working as executive producer on Kate Bush's first collection *The Kick Inside*. In fact he had been instrumental in bringing Bush to the attention of EMI when he heard some of the singer's earliest demo recordings.

144

In the run up to their next album Floyd survived another crisis, this time of the financial kind, as the company which handled their business affairs and investments collapsed. Undaunted, Floyd completed the double album *The Wall* (1979) which surprisingly peaked at number three in the UK but topped the US charts for 15 weeks. During the sessions the band hired two studios in France and travelled over two hours between the two of them to record and overdub in the two locations where they utilized more sound effects. 'That was an adventure in itself', said producer Bob Ezrin. 'We took sledgehammers to televisions, busted through doorways and went out to Edwards Air Base [in California] to record helicopters.'

The Wall, which would go on to sell over twenty million copies worldwide – and top charts in Argentina, Austria, France, Germany, New Zealand, Norway and Sweden – also spawned Floyd's first major hit single in the UK since their 1967 hit 'See Emily Play'. 'Another Brick in the Wall (Part II)' topped the UK chart for five weeks in December 1979 and hit number one in America for four weeks in March 1980. Despite this success, the single found its way on to the banned list in South Africa where the authorities deemed it was 'prejudicial to the safety of the state' as black children boycotting their schools had adopted the song as a protest anthem.

The Wall's live show which had emerged from Waters' reaction to events in Montreal nearly three years earlier debuted in Los Angeles on February 7 1980 and proved to be the most ambitious effort yet undertaken by Floyd. It involved the building of a wall 160 feet wide and 50 feet high and made up of 5lb blocks of styrofoam during the first half of the show, and then destroying it after the interval. Vastly expensive to produce, *The Wall* live was performed less than 30 times but it did lead to a two-hour movie version, directed by Alan Parker and starring Bob Geldof as 'Pink'. Premiered in London and New York in 1982, the film, which cost over $10 million, was generally panned by the critics.

Some reviewers were also less than impressed with the album with the NME asking 'Is *The Wall* the last brick in Pink Floyd's own towering edifice? Having constructed their own wall around themselves, this double album finds them rather shocked by the realization of this fact – that rock and roll is not the autonomous wonderland they assumed it to be.' The review concluded by suggesting that *The Wall* 'is the rock musicians' equivalent of the tired executive toy, a gleaming frivolous gadget that serves to occupy mid space.'

Producer Chris Thomas, however, remembers *The Wall* for another reason – his February 1980 encounter with Gilmour backstage at the band's concert at Nassau Coliseum in New York. Reflecting on the £1,000 he was paid for his work on Dark Side and its overwhelming success, he jokes, 'Every time it sells another million I have to divide a thousand pounds by another million to work out what I haven't got!' before recalling what the band's guitarist said to him before the Nassau Coliseum show. 'At the soundcheck David came over to me and said, 'You should sue us', and when I asked why, he said, 'For *Dark Side of the Moon*, you'd make millions'.'

In the run-up to the release of *The Wall* film, Floyd's original keyboard player Rick Wright left the band after a reported falling out with Waters. He was to play no part on the band's next album and in the aftermath of his departure Waters was quoted as saying, 'Now we don't pretend we're a group any more. I could work with another drummer and keyboard player very easily and it's likely that at some point I will.' At the same time Gilmour confirmed, 'None of us have ever been the best of friends. We don't get along but we're working partners.'

In the light of these comments it seemed that Pink Floyd's future was now in serious jeopardy and the band's 1983 album *The Final Cut* heralded the end of an era as Waters took centre stage. Coming a year after their *A Collection of Great Dance Songs* compilation hit the top 30 in both the US and UK, *The Final Cut* – with its strong anti-war theme – was effectively a Waters solo album in everything but name as he wrote all the songs and co-produced it with Michael Kamen.

The Final Cut was Pink Floyd's third UK chart topper, and was a number six hit in the US. It featured both Mason and Gilmour, but the latter pronounced that the album contained only three good tracks. Whether 'Not Now John' was one of them we'll never know, but the song did become only the band's fifth UK hit single during a career then spanning 16 years.

As if to confirm that Floyd were heading towards a distinctly unhappy ending, Gilmour released and went on to tour in the first half of 1984 to support his second solo album *About Face* just a few months ahead of Waters' album *The Pros and Cons of Hitch Hiking* and his world tour which featured Eric Clapton in the role of lead guitarist. In the contest between the solo albums Waters' effort climbed to number 13 in the UK and stalled at 31 in the US while Gilmour came in at number 21 in the UK and at 32 in America. Less successful was drummer Mason's second album outside Floyd, with the 1985 release *Profiles* failing to make any impression on the charts.

In the midst of the internal strife which was now overwhelming the band, *Dark Side of the Moon* was issued in the UK on the new Compact Disc format and EMI's full page newspaper advert in November 1984 included the title along with 11 others – *The Wall*, *Wish You Were Here* plus Queen and Cliff Richard albums – which were being released on CD for the first time. Two years later Dark Side became the first title pressed when EMI's UK CD plant opened in Swindon in May 1986, and when the company closed the plant in May 2002 they commemorated the occasion by pressing a limited edition of Dark Side which was presented to staff members. It came emblazoned with the words: '*Dark Side of the Moon* – First and Last – EMI Swindon 1986–2002' … and again there was no 'The'.

The animosity that had built up between Waters and Gilmour over *The Wall* and *The Final Cut* eventually produced the long anticipated official split in the ranks of Pink Floyd. After sacking Steve O'Rourke as his manager, Waters informed both EMI and CBS in December 1985 that he was no longer a member of Pink Floyd. He later admitted, 'I never wanted to be in the longest-lasting band in the history of rock 'n' roll anyway.'

Ten months later – after Waters had declared that the band was 'a spent force' creatively – he filed suit in the Chancery Division of the High Court in London in an effort to formally dissolve the partnership that was Pink Floyd and to 'protect his interest in Pink Floyd by reason of the differences between himself and Messrs Gilmour and Mason as to the ability of the individuals to continue to record and perform as Pink Floyd'.

But the other members were not finished with Pink Floyd, and wanted to release new material under that name. Waters' attempt to block Gilmour and Mason from using the name Pink Floyd was met with Gilmour telling the world, 'The three of us (Gilmour also included Wright) are very excited by the new material and we would prefer to be judged by the public on the strength of the forthcoming Pink Floyd album.' The two formal members of the band, plus their manager O'Rourke, had made clear their intention to carry on as Pink Floyd, with Wright joining them simply as a salaried musician … but without Waters.

With the legal issues still being fought over by the lawyers, Waters' 1987 tour for the album *Radio K.A.O.S.* clashed with a new Pink Floyd album and tour entitled *A Momentary Lapse of Reason* as they both played major North American dates. And this time Waters was forced to take second place as his album peaked at 25 in the UK and stalled at 50 in the US while the latest release under the banner Pink Floyd reached number three on both sides of the Atlantic.

Waters then attempted another move to block Floyd's progress by apparently threatening to stop any shows given by Pink Floyd while also claiming copyright fees for use of the inflatable flying pig he introduced to the Animals project. Finally, after Floyd responded by attaching a sizeable set of boar's genitalia to the pig – in order to distinguish it from the original sow version – an agreement was eventually reached which allowed Gilmour and Mason, plus Wright, to record and tour as Pink Floyd. In return Waters won the exclusive rights to *The Wall* and other projects.

DARK SIDE OF THE MOON REVEALED

Chapter Fourteen

A Momentary Lapse of Reason, the first album by the 'new' Waters-less three-piece Pink Floyd, was released in September 1987 and featured Gilmour, Mason and Wright plus an assortment of other musicians including bass player Tony Levin, Pat Leonard on synthesizers, and drummers Carmen Appice and Jim Keltner.

While Mason now became the only band member to play on every Floyd album, Wright's re-appearance was marked with a his name appearing in a smaller type face on the sleeve credits while Thorgerson also finally returned to the fold as sleeve designer to the Floyd after his dispute with Waters over the cover for *Animals*.

The Momentary Lapse album prompted Waters to observe of the sleeve, 'I think it's facile but quite a clever forgery', and while Gilmour responded by suggesting it was a return to top form for the band, Wright then bizarrely added, 'Roger's criticisms are fair. It's not a band album at all.'

When the Pink Floyd tour hit the UK, NME were there to review the show which played to 50,000 people packed into Wembley

Stadium in August 1988 and the music paper pronounced, 'The faceless group played note for note versions of the highlights from their 20 year career in the rock business.'

The leading music newspaper then went on to report, 'The show is spectacular but it doesn't hide the fact that what you are watching is a very up-market hi-fi – you are listening to the largest and most expensive record player in the world', before finally proclaiming, 'Pink Floyd are musically tedium incarnate and if live music means spontaneous music then you can pronounce Pink Floyd dead.'

And rivals Melody Maker were not a lot kinder. After an early mention that the 'pig's testicles are spectacular' and 'the real star' of the show, the music paper's reviewer Jonh (not a mistake) Wilde continued. 'Floyd play as ever like they are hopelessly engrossed with themselves. It doesn't reach and that's part of the idle scheme. Pink Floyd to earth. Are you receiving? The truth is we don't really know. We've just watched a giant pig fly over a football stadium and we're thinking how dumb can things get. We just gaze into space, tranced by the cosmic futility of Pink Floyd's rusty beauty. God is now officially deaf.'

Despite the views of NME and MM, Pink Floyd's popularity remained undimmed, and during a four year period beginning in 1987 they played to over six million people around the world, in venues including football grounds, an Olympic stadium, a British stately home and a floating stage in Venice's Grand Canal. Such was their appeal that in the list of top rock and pop earners for the year 1988–89, Floyd finished second with earnings of £35 million. They were behind Michael Jackson (£78 million), but ahead of The Rolling Stones (£34 million).

On the back of their top three placing for *A Momentary Lapse of Reason* (their eleventh studio album), Floyd's live follow-up, *Delicate Sound of Thunder,* peaked at number 11 in both the UK and the US, but the live album still set a new high for popular music when it became the first rock album to be played in outer space. A cassette of the album was included on the Soviet-French Soyuz 7 space mission, and both Gilmour and Mason were there at the launch in Kazakhstan in November 1988 to see their music blast off into space.

It was during the mixing of Delicate Sound of Thunder that this author went to Abbey Road Studios to speak to Gilmour about an EMI project and found himself being tested by the guitarist about various takes of his instrumental solos. Unsure of which version to use from the various recordings they made on the road, Gilmour asked me to listen to them all, spot the difference and perhaps even identify the best one – needless to say I failed to contribute anything to the process as they all sounded pretty much the same to my untrained ear.

Around the same time the unimaginable seemed to have happened when a track originally recorded by Pink Floyd on *Dark Side of the Moon* appeared in a television commercial, but it was clear from the outset that it wasn't the original album version made by the group. In 1981 the band's original version of the song 'Money' had been used in an early episode of BBC TV's comedy series *Only Fools and Horses* called 'Cash & Curry' but it was subsequently removed from later DVD releases and BBC broadcasts.

In 1989 the manufacturers of the painkiller Nurofen asked for and were given permission to use 'The Great Gig in the Sky' in a TV commercial. As composer of the song Rick Wright not only agreed to the song's use but also re-worked the track for the drug company, while original singer Clare Torry reprised her extraordinary performance from the album as the music bed for the 30-second advert. However, despite Wright's approval, it was still something that sat uncomfortably with Gilmour who was quoted as saying, 'Rick wrote the music. It's down to the writer. If my name had been on that track too it wouldn't have happened.'

While two singles from *A Momentary Lapse of Reason* made it
to the UK chart in 1987 and 1988 – On The Turning Away (#55)
and One Slip (#50) – Waters used his rights to *The Wall* to stage a
complete performance of the album on the site of the Berlin Wall in
Germany, the demolition of which had begun in November 1989.
Over 200,000 people turned out in July 1990 to see Waters, Van
Morrison, Bryan Adams, The Band and Joni Mitchell, plus actors Tim
Curry and Albert Finney in a show which was broadcast live across
the globe.

The renewed interest in the album took *The Wall – Live in Berlin*
into the UK Top 30 and the US Top 50 while in 1991 Pink Floyd
were amusingly inducted into the National Association of Brick
Distributors' Hall Of Fame in New York for services to the brick
industry. More concrete was the 20th anniversary edition of *Dark
Side of the Moon* which reached number four in Britain in 1993.

Seven years after they recorded A Momentary Lapse, Pink Floyd
released their follow up studio album and *The Division Bell* swept
to the top of the charts in both Britain and America in the spring
of 1994. In fact it was the band's fourth number one album in both
countries but while the UK list comprised the titles *Atom Heart
Mother*, *Wish You Were Here* and *The Final Cut*, the US agenda
featured *Dark Side of the Moon*, *Wish You Were Here* and *The Wall*.

A year in the studio on *The Division Bell*, with Bob Ezrin and
Gilmour sharing production credits, resulted in an album that
which topped both the US and UK charts for four weeks – replacing
Bonnie Raitt's *Longing In Their Hearts* and Mariah Carey's *Music
Box* respectively – and encouraged Ezrin to explain how his co-
producer worked. 'Dave literally went in one week on his own and
had inspiration and came back and presented it in almost finished
form to the band.'

And in an odd twist it seems that the title of the album was suggested to Gilmour by author Douglas Adams – of *Hitchhiker's Guide to the Galaxy* fame – who saw the phrase 'The Division Bell' (the name given to the bell that is rung in the British House of Commons to signal that a vote, or division, is about to take place) in the lyrics of 'High Hopes'. It was adopted at the last minute with Gilmour conceding that it 'seems to work'.

With Thorgerson in charge of cover design, which featured two giant heads with Ely Cathedral in the background, and Wright joining Gilmour as co-composer of four tracks, *The Division Bell* also introduced Gilmour's second wife, the novelist Polly Sampson, as the co-writer of lyrics on seven of the album's 11 tracks including 'Take It Back' and 'High Hopes' which were both UK top 30 hits … and the last singles to come from Pink Floyd.

In fact multi-million selling *The Division Bell* seemingly brought the curtain down on Pink Floyd's recording career as they, in the words, of Nick Mason embarked on a 'recycling business' with the live album *Pulse* topping the charts in 1995 and *Is There Anybody Out There? – The Wall Live 1980 –81* making a top twenty impact in 2001 while the four CD compilation set *Echoes – The Best Of Pink Floyd* hit the number two spot in both the UK and US.

But music – and the influence of *Dark Side of the Moon* in particular – is, it seems, never far away. In 1995, when he was on air at the BBC's London radio station Greater London Radio, Bob Harris recalls the evening that riots broke out in London's Brixton area following the death of a local black man while in police custody. On what was an altogether dark and depressing night Harris recalls how things panned out at GLR. 'We needed to find a long piece of music which we could play while the news people decided what they were going to do. Somebody asked me to find 15 to 20 minutes of music to bridge the gap before the news came back on air.'

Bizarrely, he found that he had with him in the studio something that he thought might work. 'I had Dark Side with me. I put it on and immediately I started getting calls from people who were saying how it was an eerie but darkly appropriate soundtrack to the riots.'

1995 was also the year when rumours started to circulate linking *Dark Side of the Moon* and Judy Garland's 1939 movie *The Wizard of Oz* and suggesting that there had been some sort of deliberate attempt by the band to synchronise the album with the film's audio track. The story went that if you started the album around the third roar of the MGM lion (or even just after) it would run in sync with the movie with the scarecrow's dance aligning with the track 'Brain Damage'.

Speaking a couple of years later Gilmour denied all knowledge of any intentional alignment between album and film and dismissed the idea as coming from someone 'with too much time on his hands'. Engineer Alan Parsons simply said, 'It's such a non-starter, a complete load of eyewash', while drummer Mason teased the world in 1997 when he said, 'It's absolute nonsense. It has nothing to do with The Wizard of Oz. It was all based on The Sound of Music.'

Despite these denials American singer Erykah Badu was seemingly taken with the whole *Dark Side of the Moon*-meets-The Wizard of Oz conspiracy. 'Everybody should try watching it with The Wizard of Oz. On the third roar, just push play and turn the volume down. The soundtrack goes so well with the movie. It's amazing.' Badu, who hit the UK charts with six singles and a top twenty album between 1997 and 2001, told Rolling Stone magazine by way of a postscript,, 'If you haven't tried that, you aren't a true *Dark Side of the Moon* fan. You are full of shit.'

In 2003, two years after *Echoes* almost took Pink Floyd back to the top of the charts, Steve O'Rourke, the band's manager for over 30 years suffered a massive stroke and died. Gilmour, Mason and Wright played 'Fat Old Sun' and 'The Great Gig in the Sky' at his funeral at Chichester Cathedral. A further two years on, in 2005, the world was surprised to see the three of them joined on stage by

Waters at the Live 8 concert in London's Hyde Park.

Getting the four musicians on stage for this event, held to mark the 20th anniversary of Live Aid, had apparently involved Bob Geldof talking to Mason, then to Gilmour and then to Mason again who in turn called Waters who then spoke to Geldof. The next piece in the jigsaw involved Gilmour and Waters talking for the first time in over two years before Wright was asked to join in as well.

Perhaps in the light of the famous group hug which took place at the end of the show – and made the pages of almost all the national newspapers – Waters expressed his regret about things that happened 20 years earlier. 'The argument was me rather pompously – and, I admit now, erroneously – suggesting that because I wasn't in the band anymore that the band and the band name should be retired.'

Gilmour seemed less contrite and even less enthusiastic about repeating the get-together, despite the band being offered a reported £136 million for a final tour. 'The [Live 8] rehearsals convinced me it wasn't something I wanted to be doing a lot of. I think I can fairly categorically say that there won't be a tour or an album again that I take part in' was what he told the press. He added by way of explanation, 'It isn't to do with animosity or anything that. It's just … I've been there, I've done it.'

Just a year after the Live 8 reunion, tragedy struck again for Floyd in July 2006 when the band's founding member Syd Barrett died in his home town of Cambridge aged 60. While none of the band attended Barrett's funeral service, Wright went on record to recognize his role in the band saying, 'Syd was the guiding light in the early band line-up and leaves a legacy which continues to inspire.'

In that same year the three-man Floyd (Gilmour, Mason and Wright) performed together just once at a solo Gilmour concert although Wright then joined the guitarist throughout for the whole of his three month tour. Their next – and final gig - together was perhaps appropriately at an all-star tribute to Barrett in 2007 when Waters also appeared but did not perform. The trio that had existed as Pink Floyd since 1985 was reduced to a duo in September 2008 when Wright died of cancer at the age of 65.

The New York Times obituary for Wright said that his 'spacious, somber, enveloping keyboards, backing vocals and eerie effects were an essential part of its [Floyd's] musical identity'. Gilmour added a simple and more personal note when he said, 'No-one can replace Rick Wright – he was my musical partner and my friend.'

Even though they had been signed to EMI since 1967, Pink Floyd took their record company to court in 2010 when they won an injunction barring the company from selling single downloads from the band's collection of best-selling albums. In December of the same year the Court of Appeal overturned EMI's appeal, and sided with Floyd and their argument that the record company was not allowed to sell Floyd's music in any form other than a complete album, in order to 'preserve the artistic integrity of the album.'

EMI, who admitted allowing online downloads from albums and parts of tracks to be used as ringtones, were ordered to pay the group outstanding royalties and also the costs of all the hearing which were put at £100,000. However, showing no sign of any ill-will towards their label, Pink Floyd signed a new five year deal with EMI for the UK and Europe – they were still with Columbia in the US – which confirmed that 'all legal issues between the band and the company have been settled'.

However, despite choosing to continue their long relationship with EMI, Pink Floyd found themselves on the list of artists to be sold by EMI following the company's purchase by Universal Music in 2012. In a ruling the European Commission, which allowed Universal's £1.2 billion acquisition of EMI, insisted that the new owners disposed of a list of assets in order to reduce the new company's share of the music market in Europe.

Among the assets to be sold are EMI Recordings Limited which includes the Parlophone label (but not The Beatles) and a list of artists ranging from Coldplay, Lily Allen, Kylie Minogue and Tinie Tempah through to long-serving and similarly top-selling acts such as Cliff Richard, Tina Tuner, Kate Bush, David Bowie … and Pink Floyd.

While the likes of The Rolling Stones, Queen and Robbie Williams jumped ship earlier to join Universal (and Paul McCartney moved over to Hear Records), Pink Floyd stayed loyal to EMI only to find themselves – 45 years on and 20 albums later – on somebody's shopping list.

Also in 2012, the three surviving musicians with links to Pink Floyd were all listed in the Sunday Times' Rich List of musicians with Waters at #22 (level with Rod Stewart and former Warner Music and EMI executive Roger Ames) with a fortune estimated to be worth £120 million. Gilmour and his £85 million came in ten places lower in a tie with drummers Roger Taylor (Queen) and Charlie Watts (Rolling Stones) while Mason was in at #46 on £55 million and level with the founder of Beggars Banquet Records Martin Mills.

In recent years Gilmour and Waters have appeared together just twice – firstly in July 2010 at a private charity event in Oxfordshire in front of an audience of just 200 – and then on stage at London's O2 arena in May 2011 during one of Waters' performances of *The Wall* when Gilmour once again climbed to the top of the wall to sing and play guitar just as he had twenty years earlier. And before the night was over, Mason was called from his seat in the audience to join them on tambourine for a rendition of 'Outside the Wall'.

And maybe that night in East London in 2011 will go down in history as the final performance by the surviving musicians who at various times made up the collective known as Pink Floyd. They have their place in both the US and UK Hall of Fame – they were inducted into the British version in 2005, were awarded Sweden's prestigious Polar Music Prize in 2008 for their 'monumental contribution to the fusion of art and music in the development of popular culture' and had the images from their *The Division Bell* sleeve reproduced by The Royal Mail on a set of stamps and are all set to be honoured by playright Sir Tom Stoppard whose radio play *Dark Side* Is set for broadcast on BBC Radio 2 in August 2013 to celebrate the 40th anniversary of *Dark Side of the Moon*.

Maybe after all that – plus global all-time record sales in excess of 250 million – there is nothing more for Pink Floyd to prove or achieve. In 2004 Mason wrote that while Gilmour seemed to have 'little appetite for all the ramifications of cranking up the whole machinery of touring yet again', he was not saying that it was definitely all over. 'I don't want to suggest that this is necessarily the end of Pink Floyd as an active force.'

But, despite those words, it seems that right now any new performances or recordings by the band created and named by Syd Barrett in 1965 are unlikely, although 2015 could provide the opportunity for magnificent 50th anniversary get-together.

In the meantime we can but celebrate, enjoy - and continue to analyse - the masterpiece Messrs Gilmour, Mason, Waters and Wright released in 1973 to an unsuspecting global audience who in return showered them with plaudits and prizes. There is a *Dark Side of the Moon* and while you may not be able to see it, you can still hear it.

Dark Side in View

40 individual takes on the album

'I was about ten or 11 – in 1985 or 86 – when my brother and I got to the stage of borrowing our dad's tapes to play in our bedroom and Queen was one we both liked. This was in the days of writing your own titles on the cassette box and we picked out a tape with Queen written on it. I remember vividly sitting in my brother's bedroom and putting the cassette in the player and suddenly *Dark Side of the Moon* came out of the speakers.

I remember thinking 'What on earth is this?' and being as blown away as a ten-year-old kid could be – it sounded like nothing I had ever heard before. It was the turning point when I suddenly got very interested in music – there were sounds and noises out there I had not heard before. It was so absorbing and awe-inspiring.

We admitted to dad that we had borrowed the tape and asked what it was and then we got treated to sitting down with the vinyl records and being played all of Pink Floyd properly, and *Dark Side of the Moon* remains probably my favourite album of all time.'
RICHARD WITTERICK, fan

'It remains a fresh and exciting album to listen to even after decades, and kind of underlines the historical nature of pop music. Maybe its greatest contribution is that it helped to significantly broaden the scope, subject matter and ambitions of what could be defined as rock.'
LlOYD GROSSMAN, former music writer, broadcaster and chef

'And still after all these years, fuck'n love it. It is an incredible body of music that has stood the test of time like no other.'
DON ZIMMERMANN, former President Capitol Records

'Whether we all knew that we had made an extraordinary album is the most asked question and Roger [Waters] said in print that he knew it was a mammoth work. I certainly knew it their best to date but 40 years on the charts – I didn't expect that.
I can believe that it did pass some people by in the UK but you can't escape it in America. You can't really dance to it and I have analysed it or thought about it countless times in an effort to try and repeat it. It was just well timed, well performed and well executed. I feel very proud of it. I do feel connected to it and a part of it and it certainly did me no harm as far my own career was concerned.'
ALAN PARSONS, Beatles' assistant engineer, engineer on
***Dark Side of the Moon*, producer of Pilot, Cockney Rebel, Paul McCartney and founder of The Alan Parsons Project**

'Those earlier Floyd albums – *A Saucerful of Secrets, Atom Heart Mother* and *Meddle* – were alright but *Dark Side of the Moon* was a big step and it obviously all came together and everything about it was great. There's not a lot of extra rubbish twiddling around in there ... if it was made now it would be 80 minutes. It's a great piece of work, it's a classic album that's up there. It's always going to be in the top ten of any chart that out comes out. For me it's

their classic album – as a whole it works really well, the songs are great, the links are great, the playing's great, the singing's great, the subject matter's great – it ticked all the boxes for a classic album.'
PHIL MANZANERA, Roxy Music

'It was one of Abbey Road's major achievements and it set Alan Parsons on the road to his success. It is a brilliant album and I still listen to it – not as an engineer but just for pleasure. Sgt Pepper, Abbey Road and *Dark Side of the Moon* are my three top Abbey Road albums of all time.'
KEN TOWNSEND, assistant on Beatles recordings and former head of Abbey Road Studios

'Initially I was put off by the whole prog rock thing and I didn't really listen to it properly for about ten years ands by about 1980 it was obviously boosted by *The Wall*. It is a good album and I've listened to it more in the last ten years than I did in the first ten years of its life. It sort of evokes an era – the lyrics are quite intelligent and the musicianship is good. It is a good album.'
SIR TIM RICE, Oscar/Grammy-winning lyricist, author and co-creator of *Jesus Christ Superstar, Evita* and *Chess*

'*Dark Side of the Moon* is absolutely up there in the annals of great rock albums. I would certainly have to have one of the tracks in Desert Island Discs. You sat cross-legged to listen to it and passed a joint round – and then you had another joint.'
PETER JENNER, former manager of Pink Floyd, Syd Barrett, Roy Harper and Billy Bragg

'The album was absolutely fundamental to me. I love it of course and in fact as an artist I have spent the rest of my life looking for

163

something so profound, as experimental, as moving, as ambitious. I can and do listen to it without seeing my pictures. Listen to it in its own right and I think it's a beautifully crafted album.'
IAN EMES, *Dark Side of the Moon* animator, Oscar nominee, BAFTA winner and video maker for Duran Duran, Wings, Mike Oldfield and Roger Waters

'We played it incessantly for a while at college. Girls hated it as it seemed to kill conversation. A reverential silence would descend upon the room, broken only by some bloke always pointing out that 'Money' was composed in 7/4 time signature at which point the other blokes would give lofty appreciative laugh as if to say 'You won't catch Slade doing any of that!'. But we all loved Clare Torry on 'The Great Gig in the Sky'.

It extended the possibilities of rock music. An art form originally primal and quite straightforward was now intensely complicated and carried thought processes to match. I'm not surprised it's still popular – it sounds only slightly dated. Most records you heard as a teenager tend just to reactivate feelings you had at the time but this has new associations too – both a pleasant experience.'
MARK ELLEN, writer, broadcaster and founding editor of The Word magazine

'I find it very difficult to remember my exact reaction to *Dark Side of the Moon* when it first came out. It seems to have been a major part of British rock history for ever and is still going strong. Rather like rock and roll's equivalent of the West End's The Mousetrap. I see no reason that it should not carry on in the same manner. It's already proved itself through its longevity in the charts, and as far as I can see its appeal has not become dated — as each new generation that comes along continues to buy it.

As to whether it was breaking new ground as a prog rock

concept album, it was certainly one that could claim that mantle. And it would be very difficult to deny the striking effect of the album cover, understated yet at the same time having a timeless appeal. After 40 years continuous sales who would have the temerity to deny its pedigree and its place as one of rock and roll's greatest albums.'

MIKE APPLETON, series producer, Old Grey Whistle Test and TV *In Concert* shows

'I first heard in a school common room one lunch time and my first reaction was a mixture of anticipation and thrill at the sonic soundscape. Then I purchased it (from Bakers Records in Canterbury I think) – I still have the copy – and then copied it to cassette so I could listen to it every night on headphones.

It's still breathtaking – the new mastered version sounds amazing – and for my radio series *The Record Producers*, I got access to the original multi-tracks which were truly amazing. Dark Side and also the other 1973 'concept' album masterpieces by the Temptations produced by Norman Whitfield had a profound influence on my own career as a producer. The guitar sounds – especially David's uni-vibe sound, the Nick Mason drum sound, Alan Parsons's use of echo and also the use of Leslie speakers … I've used so many of those tricks since then and to this day.

I started with 16-track in 1975 so I felt a great synchronicity to the way they worked, with both the creative freedom of 16-track but also the frustration of not having quite enough tracks.'

STEVE LEVINE, producer of Culture Club, Clash, XTC, Motorhead and chair of Music Producer's Guild

'Pink Floyd's *Dark Side of the Moon* is a masterpiece and the Prime Minister is to be commended for his taste. It is indisputably one of the great albums of British pop culture: dark, seductive, mesmerising, spacious, dynamic, weird and wonderful, composed on a vast musical canvas by a brilliant group of bold adventurous musicians and superb lyricists operating at the height of their powers.

Try to turn the clock back to the very first time you ever heard it, perhaps in a cloud of suspicious smoke. It is a recording that unfolds before you. Really pay attention to what is arguably Pink Floyd's finest accomplishment and by the time you reach the fading heartbeat in the play-out grooves, you will have been through an emotional and aesthetic wringer. Of course it probably helps if you have inhaled. Maybe someone should ask Dave about that?'
NEIL McCORMICK, Daily Telegraph chief rock critic and author

'I first heard The *Dark Side of the Moon* when I was 13 years old, some three or four years after it came out. Flicking through a friend's older brother's record collection, it stood out because of its cover. It was now the era of punk, and bands such as The Clash and The Jam had their photos on their sleeves. This was more appealing because it wasn't like that. When you opened it up, there was a poster inside with some blurred images of the band, but that was it. To an impressionable teenager it all seemed very mysterious and very adult.

The pop songs I heard on the radio or saw on TV were usually three minutes long. But I had never heard anything like this before. 'Us and Them' went on for what seemed like forever; 'On the Run' ended with what sounded like a car crash; there was a wailing woman on 'The Great Gig in the Sky', and strange snippets of conversation that drifted into earshot in between some of the tracks.

I borrowed the album and never gave it back. I played it incessantly, while poring over the lyrics.

Coming back to the album since then, the words have started to mean a lot more. What appealed to me at 13 still appeals now: whether it's the lyrics, the crashing car or David Gilmour's wonderfully overdriven guitar solo on 'Time' (though in an ideal world, I'd have knocked a minute or two off 'Us and Them'). Ultimately, the root of its appeal is that unlike the rest of us The *Dark Side of the Moon* has never grown old.'

MARK BLAKE, Q and Mojo contributor, and author of *Pigs Might Fly: The Inside Story of Pink Floyd*

'I loved the album very much as it was quite a departure from their previous recordings on which Syd obviously played a pivotal part. There's a buzz about *Dark Side of the Moon* that just seemed to connect with everybody, whatever kind of music you favoured. It became one of those 'must have' albums in your collection and there have not been many of those over the years. Still today it is a 'must have'.

It's hard to define what is groundbreaking but what they did was set new standards of recording and also making sure that their style was so definitive that it was instantly recognizable. The care and attention in making this album must have been immense. But I don't have a clue as to why it appealed to so many people – if we could answer that one, we'd all be millionaires. The timing couldn't have been better and it will be played, studied and loved in 100 years – simple as that. It will stand as a true example of one of the great genres of music dating back to its inception.'

RICK WAKEMAN, solo artist, member of the Strawbs and Yes, author and TV personality

'When in 1971 I first found the nerve to travel to the London office of Rolling Stone, I was completely intimidated. I had been doing freelance writing for the paper for months, but had never met anyone who worked for it. I walked in and there was the receptionist, braless and rolling a joint. She was, to me, impossibly hip. I could not compete.

I felt this way again two years later when The *Dark Side of the Moon* was released. It was impossibly hip. It was played on long drives or at long parties ... anywhere there was enough time to listen to the whole thing and get into the mood of it. Although Capitol Records successfully extracted 'Money' as a hit single in the United States, that was beside the point. You had to listen to the entire album to take the trip.

It had its week at number one [in the US] in 1973, but it just kept converting new listeners week after week, year after year. When it overtook Johnny's Greatest Hits by Johnny Mathis as the longest-running album ever in the American charts - Mathis having accumulated 490 weeks - I was bursting with excitement. Dark Side is still there, and we are well into the twenty-first century. As much as any album, The *Dark Side of the Moon* is a unified work. It perfectly captures a moment, and is thus eternal.

PAUL GAMBACCINI, record collector, author and broadcaster

'A friend had moved to a house in the country. *Dark Side of the Moon* had just been released, and itwas the album that was played constantly over a period of weeks, turning into months.
I can only think of it now, in sensory terms, filtered through the memories of that time. The rituals of crumbling hash and tobacco into rolling papers on the sleeve, a group of friends who would soon be going our separate ways, impossible as it seemed at the time. Oddly, I have no memory of being particularly affected by the album's theme of madness; it seemed almost incidental; it was the feelings the music evoked - the sense of dreamy spaciousness, of transport, rather than the meanings stated in the lyrics that struck home so forcibly. It felt like a very important record at that time; important in rock music and in my own small world.

But it's not my favourite Floyd album, and its phenomenal success seemed to infect the group with a kind of gigantism. The records that came after *Dark Side of the Moon* feel bloated and overly conceptual. I always loved the Floyd's ballads most of all – that sense of psychedelic pastoralism. Playing 'Us and Them' now, I see myself sitting in that house in the country, in a state of suspended animation, enveloped in a bittersweet feeling of melancholia and yearning, looking out through leaded windows onto an English garden, where it has started to rain. And the lunatic is on the grass...'

MICK BROWN, former Rolling Stone and Sunday Times writer, Daily Telegraph feature writer and author of *Tearing Down the Wall of Sound: The Rise And Fall Of Phil Spector*

'My awareness of the rock mainstream when Dark Side first appeared, as I headed hesitantly for the joys of teenagedom, had more to do with Free and the Faces than the Floyd. That was chiefly because back then, you could still listen to pop radio without developing an urgent need to take a sledgehammer to the transistor, and partly because albums simply cost too much pocket money. We were in the early stages of learning that music could sound pretty good at 33rpm as well as 45.

Those pop stations of the time would never pay daytime attention to anything as serious as a concept album, so my initial familiarity with Dark Side was probably limited to the occasional outing for 'Money' in any TV or radio piece about the financial crisis. Plus ça change.

But as a longtime chart-watcher even by 1973, I was soon conscious of Dark Side as a constant presence in the UK album chart for the next several years. This from a band who, bafflingly to a pop fan, would have nothing to do with the singles scene.

When I became acquainted with a mythical American magazine called Billboard, for which I would go on to write regularly, I could only offer respect to any album that had apparently taken up life membership of the magazine's fabled top 200 chart. A properly informed opinion of Dark Side didn't really follow until quite a bit later, when I began to interview Messrs Gilmour and Waters, and later still Wright and Mason.

For all its weighty reputation, the record seems to have surprisingly little of the self-congratulatory pomp of its arty 1970s contemporaries. Instead, it retains a certain magisterial calm, not to mention some nifty tunes and harmonies. Needless to say, we'll still be going on about it when the next anniversary rolls around, and the next.'

PAUL SEXTON, music journalist and broadcaster

'Well, without pouring any more acid on the situation I think we all know by now from various satellites that the dark side of the moon is as featureless as the side that presents itself to planet earth today. Nobody has any lights on back there, except a family of Clangers and a Soup Dragon.

But you have to admire any musician that thinks less is more particularly when they make as much money as Roger Waters. If anything they all should be congratulated on being the first to discover the minimalist period before Soft Cell and the 80's, and the 'One Note Samba' which actually has more chords. Accordingly, Waters' musicians are dutifully nailed to the stage rather like nude models at the Windmill Theatre in London's 50's. Play, but don't move around. Hence the name 'Water's Handle Music', rather than Handel's 'Water ...oh never mind...' At least it had more life in it than a deaf sausage and Leonard Cohen thrown down Oxford Street.

Modal was done way before Pink Floyd by way of monk's chants and Celtic music. Pink Floyd's music can be as boring as accountancy depending upon what planet you're on. Actually, I would assume accountancy is a lot more interesting than watching paint dry. At least with accountancy you get coffee breaks and two hours for lunch. Back in the late 60s my contemporaries referred to Pink Floyd as 'slit your wrist music'. It's definitely not challenging stuff.

If only Roger could have kept up with the likes of Syd Barrett and Richard Wright he could have at least come up with some halfway decent tunes. The album happened at the right time, same as most things in life.'

KEITH EMERSON, member of The Nice and ELP, and solo artist.

'In the 70s we were still in a predominantly audio world, but it was a two-dimensional one. Yes, we had stereo at home and in our cars and recordists were using the new horizon to spread out their ideas. But Dark Side went far beyond the left/right axis. It was a four-dimensional experience: it had height, width and depth; but it also had a fourth dimension of surreal imagination. It was an aural acid trip, blowing away the boundaries of reality and taking us to places we had never been before with popular music – all held together by beautifully crafted, lyrically profound and accessible songs perfectly performed and recorded. It was the fulfillment of a promise first made by the Beatles in their ambitious productions – which along with the recordings of Spike Jones, the Goons and Firesign Theatre were what moved me to become a producer. But somehow Dark Side was deeper and more meaningful than anything I had ever heard before. I was intimidated by it, inspired by it, addicted to it. And I shared my passion for it with absolutely everyone I knew.'

BOB EZRIN, producer of Alice Cooper's *Billion Dollar Babies* album (which was knocked off #1 in US by *Dark Side of the Moon*), who also produced Kiss, and Pink Floyd albums *The Wall*, *A Momentary Lapse of Reason* and *The Division Bell*

'I was a massive fan of all their early records up to and including

Meddle and Obscured by Clouds but I really didn't like *Dark Side of the Moon* when I first heard it. To me, at that time, it felt like they'd sold out! However, over the years I've grown to appreciate it although it's still not one of my favourites.

However it did break new ground re: production but I'm not so convinced regarding composition and it had no real impact on me as a musician. I think its success was because it was a very different/original record for the time but with enough melodic content for it to be accepted by the masses, and it is probably up there with all the great landmark albums.'

CHRIS HUFFORD, co-manager of Radiohead and former member of EMI band Aerial FX

'At the time I was still hoping that the Beatles' spirit could be continued so that all their groundbreaking work did not become unravelled, so I felt saddened by Floyd's work. However current events circa 2012 show that Floyd were on top of their game 40 years ago and were seeing the world as it really is – the culmination of 40–100 years of planning for the formation of a totalitarian state. So Floyd possibly knew what was coming.

At the time I thought, 'What an easy gig for a bassist like me.' The music itself is very easy to play and I would have enjoyed its self-indulgence immensely at the time. Pink Floyd's music and lyrics stand up as it comes from good hearts and truth searchers. Floyd's morals are intact.'

GORDON HASKELL, member of Les Fleurs De Lys and King Crimson, and solo singer/songwriter

'Some definitive albums such as The Beatles' Sgt Pepper, The Beach Boys' *Pet Sounds* and Elton John's Goodbye *Yellow Brick Road* made an immediate impression on me but I had to listen to *Dark Side of the Moon* quite a few times before I realised its full potential.

Its release came after my first-ever trip to the USA and by the time of my second trip later in the same year it had given them their first No. 1 album in the US. I was somewhat surprised to find that, despite their previous great success in the UK, they had not had more impact in the States before.'

JEFF GRIFFIN, producer BBC Radio 1 and *In Concert* radio series, concert coordinator Live Aid

'I loved it but as I'd heard it taking shape wafting down the corridor (at Abbey Road) and with occasional playbacks in the room, it was not so much of a surprise when I finally got a copy home except hearing it all together as if it's one song. The full range sound and use of dynamics set new standards. The girls' voices are very 'soul' and all sounded like perfect blending of soul/rock yet in a very English way.

I have used it sometimes as a studio speaker test record! And also in production and arrangement to learn that less is more. Its success is down to the fact that it is a good record and bears repeated playing. It was released in the 'golden years' of the LP record. It had a great cover and everyone had heard of Pink Floyd by the time of Dark Side and they had high kudos. I'd put it midway in my top ten.

Dark Side was their eighth album so they knew what they were doing and now believed in the song rather than the 'experiment' which some of their earlier material was guilty of.'

JOHN LECKIE, Abbey Road studios, engineer on *Meddle* and producer of The Stone Roses, Radiohead, The Verve, New Order

'I have no memory whatsoever of buying *Dark Side of the Moon* as I used to buy and blag loads of albums at the time. By 1973 I was working at Warner Brothers as a record plugger and we used to swap promo copies with a lot of people in other record companies,

173

but I am sure I bought this one as I had been collecting all their albums since *Piper at the Gates of Dawn*. *Dark Side of the Moon* was just the next album so I would have bought it on release and played it at home on my expensive Teac hi-fi on huge Wharfedale speakers. It had great packaging too with postcards and posters, all of which I kept in pristine condition in the sleeve – no pinning them to the walls for me. It all took on more significance later when I ran the Harvest label and I watched them trying to work out how to follow this mega success.'

MARK RYE, former Harvest label manager

'I probably liked it so much because most of it was instrumental – that was what appealed to me. I would have been about 12 when I first heard it.

I could listen to it over and over again – it is the one album that I listen to the whole way through every time, I don't skip a track. Originally it was just the music and then followed by understanding some of the lyrics. The lyrics actually make me smile – they are quite cheeky in a way and I think they are laughing at life.

It's all about work work work. It is a miserable, despairing piece but you can sing along to it. My children were brought up on it and my sons still sing along to it.

I used to work for an optician and for me a prism was all about altering light in some way and it was pretty colours, but if you asked most people what they know about Floyd they would come up with the cover artwork for Dark Side. You could put the sleeve down and people would instantly recognise it even if they didn't know the album or the band.

Not bothered at all that they are anonymous and don't do interviews because it's all about the music for me – if I can have the music then the rest of it's irrelevant. They are pretty selfish as far as the fans go because fans like to have some kind of connection.

174

But it hasn't put me off them and their music. The fact that they sold and still sell millions without all the usual pomp and circumstance speaks volumes for their music.

It is near the top of my collection of Floyd records but Division Bell is their best for me – but I can listen to *Dark Side of the Moon* whatever mood I'm in. I've got about six copies of it and I can take them with me.

It's an album that we do take on holiday with us to play when we are away and I also iron to it.'
LORRAINE MASON, fan

'EMI would never have been generous to have given me a sample copy. I would have had to take one from the boxes I had bought to listen to. I liked it obviously and it seemed to be a continuation of where they were heading anyway – it struck me that it had a bit more of a commercial edge to it than the earlier ones. I knew all their other records but for a lot of people it would have been the first Floyd record they heard and bought.

Maybe it was just a child of its time – I used to sell a lot to students who would have probably listened to it with a joint. Whether it was a record where people were looking for something better than much of the 70s pop music – maybe it was as a breath of fresh air and maybe the timing helped it.

It would have been a must-have with the student population at the start of prog rock. It was shrink wrapped with a sticker giving the band's name and the album title.'
ANDY GRAY, founder Andy's Records shops and head of BGO Records

'As a child of the late 50s I knew who Pink Floyd were, as I had an older brother and sister who played their albums. I was a Floyd fan even then. It wasn't pop music but living in the North East it somehow made it exciting to hear music that was coming up from London.

I tingled all over when I heard Dark Side – I just couldn't believe it because I thought *Meddle* was good and listening to *Dark Side of the Moon* and 'The Great Gig in the Sky' in particular which was just wonderful.

It was all about tragedy and doom but perhaps that was because I was an impressionable 15-year-old. I didn't think it was prog rock but it was certainly pomp rock.

I had no idea what they looked like and it didn't matter, and it was probably because everything was focused on the music. It was probably sometime in the late 1970s before I actually saw what they looked like. There was no need to know because the music just overpowered you.

I bought a copy after borrowing one from a friend – my brother wouldn't let me borrow his. I saved up my pocket money – it was a lot of money I remember and my pocket money was about 50p – and I went out and bought it, and just played it non-stop. I still regularly listen to it about once a month.

I went to a church youth club in the North East and we often played it on the record player in the club although the vicar thought it was all very stupid – we sat cross-legged on the floor and listened to it. There was probably something of a secret society between us kids and everybody just thought *Dark Side of the Moon* was wonderful.

At my wedding we had Floyd's 'Shine On You Crazy Diamond' before I walked down the aisle and 'Breathe In The Air' from *Dark Side of the Moon* was played while we signed the register, and it's probably still my top Floyd album.'
BLANCHE BANGAY, fan

'I first saw Pink Floyd as a spotty 14 year old at the Central Hall, Chatham in 1967. Roll on six years to the release of *Dark Side of*

the Moon… by which time Floyd had a momentum and power
that was of Superliner proportions. You couldn't ignore them any
longer. They had seized the zeitgeist by the scruff and created the
most complete album since Sgt Pepper … indeed, probably EVER.
The converging lines of IT crossed at the point that album was
created. Like the Beatles … the sum of the parts overshadowed the
individual contributions. Storm's sleeve is genius in its simplicity
(why didn't we think of that?). Alan Parsons' sonic contribution is
immense. And, of course, the music, arrangements and production
of the band is incredible – they all clearly played their part.
But the primary magic for me comes in the cocktail of Roger's
provocative poetry and Dave's soaring guitar and haunting vocals –
a (tad rocky) marriage made in a moon-filled heaven.

I think *Dark Side of the Moon* was responsible for slowing time
down in the 70s before punk came and speeded it all up again …
the resultant increase in dope sales was inversely proportional to
the velocity that people could operate. Dark side of the room. Big
cushions. Joss-tticks. Those were the days. And, guess what? It still
sounds amazing today even with a clean drug test.'
**KEITH PEACOCK, Peacock Design, sleeve designers for Kate
Bush, Iron Maiden and Simply Red**

'I remember playing through it and thinking, 'Mmmmm'. I like
really commercial songs and the only song that really stood out for
me was 'Money' and you couldn't play it on the radio because of
the word 'bullshit'. I don't think you can even play it today during
daytime Radio 2 as we featured *Dark Side of the Moon* on an Easter
Monday show in 2012 featuring the best-selling albums of all time
and I wanted to play 'Money' but I was told you can't play it on
Radio 2 in the afternoon.

(**Dark Side of the Moon* was #8 on that Radio 2 Top 40 best-
selling albums list)

I thought it was interesting as a concept album but I didn't really get excited. Somebody from EMI gave me a white label of it and I sort of liked 'Arnold Layne' and 'See Emily Play' and thought it might be some more of that – but no.

Then I started to listen to it a bit more and thought the production was really good and thought maybe it's not so bad after all – it sort of crept up on me.

I don't get 33 million sales – not at all. It was pretty miserable. I knew who they were and was quite interested in their music. The album sleeve was quite effective but in truth it's 'great sleeve, shame about the album'. I thought that perhaps it was a bit of 'the king's new clothes' – that it was the thing to do to like it. That did happen quite a bit and people did buy albums because it was a hit.

I collected every single and album that was in the charts, and did go and buy a finished copy even though I had a white label and foolishly I dumped the white label which would have been quite valuable.

It does have a place in rock history if only because of its huge sales and the re-issues. It is an album where you spot different things each time you hear it, but I never really got it and began to wonder if it was just me.'

PHIL SWERN, producer, songwriter, music collector and producer of BBC Radio 2's *Pick of the Pops* and *Sounds of the 60s*.

'I first heard *Dark Side of the Moon* performed live by Pink Floyd at the Rainbow Theatre in Finsbury Park on February 17 1972 [a full 12 months before the album was released], and went back the next night because I enjoyed it so much. I managed this not through the good offices of the Floyd themselves, who were notoriously unwilling to accommodate music writers, but through the kindness of the manager of the theatre, John Morris, a friend of mine who had given me a pass that read: 'Admit to all parts of the theatre at all times'.

It's not often that a lengthy piece of music, heard for the first time, makes much of an impact on me but Dark Side sounded great first time around. It helped that I found myself a seat on a lighting rig that was suspended from the circle, so I looked down on the band with nothing to obstruct my view, and during the show someone passed me the kind of cigarette that isn't generally available at street-corner tobacconists, but even without this helpful attitude adjuster, I just knew that music the Floyd were playing was going to be massively popular, though I couldn't have guessed how popular.

The first time I heard the album was about 12 months later when EMI launched it with a listen-in at the London Planetarium, quite an appropriate choice of venue. The Floyd didn't turn up, of course, and instead sent cardboard cut-outs of themselves to stand in the foyer and greet their guests. The LP was played at terrific volume through a state-of-the-art sound system and when all those alarm clocks went off everyone jumped.

I have since played Dark Side 387 times (well, that's a guess) and haven't become bored. In Nicholas Schnaffner's Floyd biography *Saucerful of Secrets* I am quoted as saying that the reason for its success is because the album is the perfect accompaniment to sexual congress. 'It's a great record to fuck to,' I told Nicholas. 'Especially side one, climaxing as it does with 'The Great Gig in the Sky' and Clare Torry's orgasmic shrieks, sobs and moans. Millions of people across the globe have fucked to *Dark Side of the Moon*.' My opinion has not changed.'

CHRIS CHARLESWORTH, NME and MM writer, author and now managing editor of Omnibus Books

'My main memory of *Dark Side of the Moon* is not buying it or even listening to it, but the insert poster. I was at university at the time and every student flat you went in had the pyramid poster on the wall, and more than likely the famous poster of the female tennis player scratching her bum on the other. It was the image of the time. The album was ubiquitous as well, echoing down every student stairwell and corridor preceded by that sweet smoky smell ….of success.'

JON WEBSTER, former MD, Virgin Records, and, CEO, Music Manager's Forum

'It still sends a shiver down the spine every time I hear it. It is undoubtedly one of the great rock albums of all time – it was a piece of pure genius.

The album was shrink wrapped and stickered and they were famous enough to get away without putting their name and the title on the cover in a traditional sense.'

MARTIN NELSON, EMI, CBS and Universal Records.

'I was born around the year it came out and was aware of certain things on it – 'Great Gig in the Sky' was on a Nurofen TV ad in the late 80s, and 'Money' was in an episode of Only Fools and Horses. My brother was ten years older than me and he was been playing it and I remember hearing things like the beginning of 'Time' and 'Money'.

I listened to it of my own accord when I was about 16 or 17 and was into hip-hop at the time. There was a big rave culture with lots of drugs about and older brothers were into Floyd and younger brothers were into rave and they swapped music. I got a tape copy of *Dark Side of the Moon* and really got into to it, and outside of rave and black music Floyd were the band I got into.

Things like Floyd would often be listened to next day when people were coming down after a rave – it was perceived as being sort of stoned music and what you would put on the following morning when you were trying to get to sleep. Lots of ravers had a sort of hippy side to them and *Dark Side of the Moon* was psychedelia. I don't find it particularly depressing but at times their music was a bit grim.

I had a bunch of school friends who I introduced it to, got them to check it out. You could put *Dark Side of the Moon* on and just leave it without ever skipping a track – someone would just get up and turn it over while everyone got stoned. As albums go it is a very good album, there aren't many great albums out there but this one – there isn't a track that you skip. You can take whatever you want from the lyrics.

I liked the sleeve concept – it was appropriate as we thought the music was deep and profound and the cover could be everything and nothing – it didn't tell you anything about the music or the band.

The cover was kind of anti-commercial which I did find attractive in a way. It is an eternal cover that goes on for ever – it is iconic. One of the attractions is the way it looked, and that has nothing to do with what comes out of the speakers, but you could tie up connections if you wanted. People can read all kinds of things in to it.

When I got into records I wanted as early a copy of *Dark Side of the Moon* as I could afford in order to listen to it, and I got an very early copy but not a first copy, and it's as close to *Dark Side of the Moon* when it came out as I can get.'

IAN RYAN, fan

'The first time I heard the album in its entirety was in Abbey Road studios, sitting with the band listening to it. It was incredibly impressive. Immediately it leapt out at you as a departure in some way, something very special. The first thing that struck me was the phenomenal quality of *Dark Side of the Moon*, Dave's voice and guitar, the lushness of the sound – it was a giant stepping stone and it was a concept. It was the first album that was a concept album and that was why we had all these bits, the whole thing was a concept. But I'm not a Pink Floyd fan now – I listen to country music and opera – but I can tell you that the last time I heard *Dark Side of the Moon* was in Ibiza at an exhibition of my album cover art four years ago, and they played *Dark Side of the Moon* non-stop and I thought, 'What a brilliant album'.'

AUBREY 'PO' POWELL, *Dark Side of the Moon* sleeve designer, co-founder of Hipgnosis

'Dark Side was an anticipated record and I do distinctly remember getting it and listening to it for the very first time and being super into it, and not only for the music but for the actual sonic aspect – I was a hi-fi fan. The moment when the guitar switches from the radio sound to the big hi-fi sound – I haven't listened to the record for years but certain moments from it just stick in your brain.

We all just sat there and thought 'How did they do this?' – you'd replay moments in order to try and figure out was going on in the mix. It is one of the most important records ever sonically, quite apart from its quire extraordinary musical and lyrical value – sonically alone it gets an award.'

PETER ASHER, member of Peter & Gordon, artist manager and producer of James Taylor, Linda Ronstadt and Bonnie Raitt

'I remember very clearly at the age of 13 going round to my next door neighbour who had just bought the album when it came out. To be honest I found Dark Side a little soft and safe in comparison to that *Saucerful of Secrets* freakout which I thought was then the classic Floyd sound. I don't think I got the concept but what did stick with me were the sound effects and the synth on 'On the Run'. The sound of the album is attractive and radio-friendly in a way *Ummagumma* certainly wasn't. It is still one of the all time greats for the way it influenced music and musicians but like the Beatles' Sgt Pepper, for the Floyd fan it is almost too familiar.'

RICK BENBOW, keyboard player with Brit Floyd

'I don't remember the first time I heard the album, it kind of became part of the soundscape, part of the fabric, quite organic. Pink Floyd always set new standards, explored new areas and themes and *Dark Side of the Moon* is a magnificent record, a wondrous journey, still rolling on!!'
JOHN FIDDLER, Medicine Head

'Many serious students, critics and lovers of rock music still believe, as I do, that it remains an unparalleled musical triumph.'
BHASKAR MENON, former President, Capitol Records and Chairman, EMI Music.

'It really is right up there in the list of all time great rock albums – it would certainly be in my top ten, and probably in my top five. You can play it a lot of times and each time you discover something new and that's quite a skill with any record, and even ten years after its release, people were being intrigued by *Dark Side of the Moon* which has constantly reinvigorated itself. And the fact it never reached number one in the UK is part of the myth, and its run in the US chart added to the strength of the album and its overall uniqueness.'
BOB HARRIS, presenter, *Sounds of the Seventies* and *The Old Grey Whistle Test*

DARK SIDE OF THE MOON REVEALED

ACKNOWLEDGEMENTS

The author wishes to thank all those people who kindly gave up their time to be interviewed and agreed to share their memories of DSOM with me - albeit 40 years on. Thanks as ever must also go to the the British Library (keep it free!) and back issues of Melody Maker, New Musical Express,.Sounds, Q, Music Week and Billboard plus an assortment of helpful and informative websites dedicated to Pink Floyd and a host of other music subjects.

Finally many thank yous to Mark Neeter at Ovolo/Clarkesdale books for all his support and help plus the editors and designers who make things happen - all your efforts are much appreciated

BIBLIOGRAPHY

Inside Out – A Personal History of Pink Floyd by Nick Mason (Phoenix, 2005)

Pigs Might Fly: The Inside Story of Pink Floyd by Mark Blake (Aurum Press, 2008)

The Dark Side of the Moon by John Harris (Harper Perennial, 2006)

Saucerful of Secrets – The Pink Floyd Odyssey by Nicholas Schnaffner (Sidgwick & Jackson, 1991)

Inside The Record Industry by Clive Davis (William Morrow, 1974)

The Rough Guide to Pink Floyd by Toby Manning (Rough Guides, 2006)

Pink Floyd by Patrick Humphries (Chameleon, 1997)

Echoes: The Complete History of Pink Floyd by Glenn Povey (Mind Head Publishing, 2007)

The Billboard Book of Number One Albums by Craig Rose (Billboard Books, 1996)

Complete Guide to the Music of Pink Floyd by Andy Mabbett (Omnibus, 1995)

London Live by Tony Bacon (Balafon Books, 1999)

Off the Record by Joe Smith (Pan Books, 1990)

White Bicycles by Joe Boyd (Serpent's Tail, 2007)

Index